Build Your Own PC Recording Studio

Jon Chappell

McGraw-Hill/Osborne

New York   Chicago   San Francisco   Lisbon   London   Madrid   Mexico City
Milan   New Delhi   San Juan   Seoul   Singapore   Sydney   Toronto

The **McGraw·Hill** Companies

McGraw-Hill/Osborne
2100 Powell Street, Floor 10
Emeryville, California 94608
U.S.A.

To arrange bulk purchase discounts for sales promotions, premiums, or fund-raisers, please contact **McGraw-Hill**/Osborne at the above address. For information on translations or book distributors outside the U.S.A., please see the International Contact Information page immediately following the index of this book.

Build Your Own PC Recording Studio

1234567890 QPD QPD 019876543

ISBN 0-07-222904-7

Publisher	**Proofreader**
Brandon A. Nordin	*John Gildersleeve*
Vice President & Associate Publisher	**Indexer**
Scott Rogers	*Robert J. Richardson*
Acquisitions Editor	**Computer Designers**
Marjorie McAneny	*Tabitha M. Cagan, Lucie Ericksen*
Project Editor	**Illustrators**
Elizabeth Seymour	*Melinda Lytle, Michael Mueller, Lyssa Wald*
Acquisitions Coordinator	**Cover Series Design**
Tana Allen	*Ted Holladay*
Copy Editor	**Cover Illustration**
Bart D. Reed	*Ted Holladay*
Technical Editor	
F.F. Francis	

This book was composed with Corel VENTURA™ Publisher.

This book is dedicated to my children:
Jen, Katie, Lauren, and Ryan (music-hounds and gadget-fiends all)
who keep me fresh and fill me with hope;
and to their mother, my wife, Mary, who remains my reason
for booting up in the morning.

About the Author

Jon Chappell is a multi-style guitarist, composer, and arranger. He studied guitar under Carlos Barbosa-Lima at Carnegie Mellon University, and then earned his master's degree in music composition from DePaul University. He has served as editor-in-chief of *Guitar Magazine,* and was the founder and first editor-in-chief for *Home Recording* magazine. Jon is the author of several books, including *Guitar for Dummies, Rock Guitar for Dummies, The Recording Guitarist: A Guide for Home and Studio, Digital Home Recording,* and *The Gig Survival Guide.* He has written extensively for *Keyboard, EQ, Guitar Player, Electronic Musician, Onstage, Drum!, Rolling Stone,* and the *New York Times,* and has recorded with Pat Benatar, Judy Collins, Graham Nash, and Bruce Springsteen.

In his home studio, Jon composes and produces music for film, TV, and radio. He has contributed to such shows as National Public Radio's *All Things Considered, Walker, Texas Ranger, All My Children, Guiding Light, Northern Exposure, B. Smith with Style,* and the feature film *Bleeding Hearts,* directed by actor/dancer Gregory Hines. He lives in the New York City area and can be reached at http://jonchappell.com.

Contents

Acknowledgments

I'd like to extend my gratitude to several people who helped make this book a reality. First, to my acquisitions editor at McGraw-Hill/Osborne Media Group, Margie McAneny, whose vision paved the way for the creation of this project, and who provided wise counsel and constant inspiration through all stages of its production. Thanks also to the following folks at OMH: Tana Allen, my project coordinator, for keeping me on track; Lyssa Wald, for expert art supervision and aesthetic guidance; marketing manager Kate Viotto and publicity manager Bettina Faltermeier for their tireless efforts to keep the BYO series front and center in the public eye; Ted Holladay, for the ultra-cool cover design; Elizabeth Seymour, my project editor, who upholds the top-notch production standards established by Osborne/McGraw-Hill; and Jean Butterfield, for the excellent page layout design that makes these books such an inviting experience.

Thanks to Brian McConnon of Steinberg and to Chris Douglass of Edirol for their technology support and advice. Thanks to Craig Anderton, whose grasp of the technological is exceeded only by his ability to create great music with it. And a very special thanks goes out to Emile Menasché, for allowing me to benefit from his friendship, humor, and peerless expertise in digital audio software.

Introduction

Any new computer that you buy these days can have you recording music, downloading and playing MP3s, and ripping your own CDs right out of the box. In fact, you can do a lot with just your computer's internal components. But what do you do when you want to take the next step? How do the pros—aspiring or established—approach serious music-making on the computer? What goes on in their world and how can you create music the way they do?

Build Your Own PC Recording Studio starts by answering these questions and then takes you through your first recording, editing, and mastering session—and beyond. Together, we'll embark on a journey that starts inside a basic PC and ends up, if not on the pop charts, at least on your home entertainment system.

This book is written for technologically comfortable enthusiasts who want to build their own system to take advantage of the same powerful tools enjoyed by singer-songwriters, instrumentalists, sound designers, video scorers, and producers. For audio pros, the computer is a serious music-making tool, not just a box for gaming, word processing, and Web surfing.

In this book, you'll not only assemble an affordable computer that's optimized for audio production, you'll learn why we make the choices we do when selecting components, peripherals, software, and even furniture! Every selection discussed offers insight into what benefit our choices have toward creating music and audio.

I've structured the book in three parts. Part I introduces the world of digital audio, as seen from the pros' point of view, and how it relates to affordable and accessible technology—a home computer you can easily build yourself in an afternoon. There's nothing technical here, just the background of how computers came to be the tool of choice for today's music makers, and how you can use your PC to perform all the stages involved in a recording project.

Part II is where we roll up our sleeves and actually build the system that will do everything from capturing songwriting ideas to producing multitrack audio projects and finished CD masters sporting commercial spit 'n' polish. We'll select and hook up essential audio peripherals that will help control our system and act as valuable input devices for our creative impulses. And then we'll install and configure the software that'll enable you to build a full-blown arrangement with all the fixin's. In Chapters 4 and 5, we construct an arrangement the way the pros do, using the software and music peripherals that are common to home and pro studios.

I've selected Cubase SX as the primary project software because of its incredible versatility, user-friendly interface, and ubiquitous use in the professional audio-recording industry. I highly recommend you purchase this software, but to build the arrangements in this book, you only need download the demo from Steinberg.net and follow right along. If you like the experience, you can decide to purchase the software later. Cubase SX is cross-platform, so Macintosh users can also follow the project-building sections step by step. Another bonus: If you find you're having trouble producing the audio tracks from scratch in Chapters 4 and 5, you can download the prerecorded tracks from my Web site, www.jonchappell.com. There's a feedback forum there, too, in case you want to take me to task or shower me with adoring superlatives.

It's important to realize that a tricked-out computer does not a home studio make. And so I've devoted Part III to converting a generic workspace into a creative environment for music-making. I cover easy do-it-yourself projects for sound treatment, speaker placement, and home-studio ergonomics. You needn't be a physics major or a licensed carpenter; you just have to love music enough to want it to sound great, and you have to get to know your home-center sales personnel by their first names. When you finish Part III, you will have created a space that fairly screams "Music made here!"

Although I've focused on the PC and Windows for the project computer, Macintosh users will also benefit from *Build Your Own PC Recording Studio* because the steps in Part II are virtually identical on the Mac version of Cubase SX as they are on the PC, and the home studio tips in Part III are "hardware agnostic" as well. Plus, everyone in this day and age should be "bi-platform." Windows XP and Mac OS X have learned a lot from each other over the years, and for the user, making the transition is seamless—especially when virtually all hardware peripherals and most software work on both platforms.

It is my sincere hope that you not only learn how to build a PC-based recording studio from this book, but that you gain insight into the fascinating world of pro-level music-making and recording and that you bring out the creative potential that lurks within you. The best part of this whole endeavor occurs when the music starts flowing, all your impulses are true, and the tools are just there to speed the process along. Enjoy!

—Jon Chappell

Part I

Building Your Recording Studio

Chapter 1

A Recording Studio in a Box

As computers evolve, they become more user friendly, more flexible in what they can do, and more powerful in how they do it. But nowhere is this progress more spectacularly evident than in recording music and audio. Computers have been able to record music for some time, but now it's so ridiculously easy that what used to be the exclusive province of audio professionals has fallen into the hands of home hobbyists. Because the process has gotten cheaper as well as easier, even non-technical people have the potential to create the same master-quality work that professionals do.

There are two reasons for the successful relationship of computers and music, apart from computers making *everything* increasingly easier: one, music recording is a digital process, and computers speak fluent digital; two, the format that is the eventual destination for the majority of recorded music—the commercial CD—has remained unchanged since its inception in 1983 and is unlikely to change anytime soon (even with the introduction of higher-resolution formats, such as DVD-Audio and SACD [Super Audio Compact Disc], which are slowly coming onto the scene). It's as if you got a salary increase every year but inflation, the cost of living, and your rent remained the same. As long as the CD stays put (with respect to format), the technology to create one will become even cheaper and easier to use over time.

So good have computers become at the recording process that it's now possible to perform *all* the steps in the recording chain within one box, rather than having to employ a separate machine for each of the tasks in the chain: multitrack recording, mixing, applying effects, mastering, and burning a CD. What's more, you don't have to be a technological genius—or do you call them "geeks"?—to configure a computer for pro-level recording duties. To build a PC-based recording studio involves little more technical ability than installing a few peripherals in the computer's interior and following the dialog box prompts in the software installation discs.

If the part about going into your computer's innards scares you, don't let it. Yes, once upon a time only the most technically minded would dare to open Pandora's Box (i.e., their computer case) and risk voiding the warranty, damaging the sensitive and precariously installed circuitry, and even incurring electrical shock. But these days, *computers are made to be opened by their users.* You'd be expected to do it anyway if you were installing a video card, a FireWire or SCSI card, additional RAM, a second hard drive, and so on. So get used to "going into the box."

If you're really not comfortable with doing anything inside your computer, that's fine, too. You can have a friend do it or even a qualified service person. The disadvantage of having a service person install components, of course, is that he'll charge you for it. The advantage is that the work comes with a warranty, so if anything doesn't work right after the procedure, you usually have some recourse.

At the same time, although this book assumes you're not squeamish about opening up your computer, you should know that the procedures involved are extremely simple. If you can assemble a cube with LEGO blocks, you can perform most of the hardware-installation routines discussed in these pages. There's no soldering involved, no fancy tools to buy, and most important, nothing dangerous to you or your computer. If you're ever in doubt, you can always back out at any time and restore your machine to its previous state.

The Computer as Command Central

A computer is not only capable of capturing your inspired flights of musical fancy (i.e., your rippin' death metal riffs), it provides the best means for controlling and manipulating those riffs after the fact. In addition to the hardware inside the computer that magically manipulates the ones and zeros magnetically imprinted on your hard drive, the computer's interface (the screen, keyboard, and mouse) offers up a galaxy of wonderful windows, graphic displays, buttons, sliders, and other controls for viewing and altering the data. And all of those tweaks you make onscreen come back into the analog world as transformed (and hopefully much improved) music.

The computer's greatest contribution is not in its abilities as a "data bucket," but what you can do once the material is safely inside. Figure 1-1 gives examples of just some of the different types of environments that exist for manipulating music once it's in digital form.

Figure 1-1
Three windows showing different ways to view and control a musical passage: in an arrangement with other parts (top left), on the waveform level (bottom left), and in a virtual mixer environment (right).

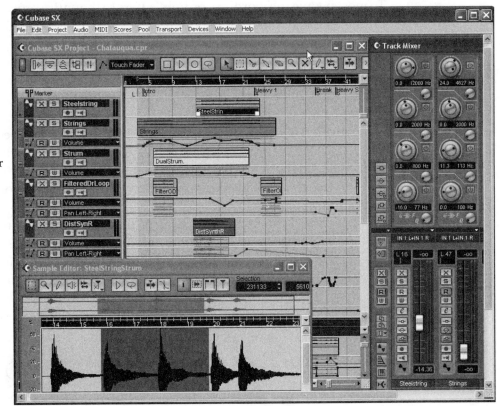

The Digital Audio Recording Process

Virtually all recording is done digitally and can therefore be easily integrated into computer tasks. Though some analog recording still goes on, most of the world now records music digitally—and of course anything on a CD has been through the digital process at least at the end of the line. So where traditional recording involves a mix of machines and technologies, computer-based music production keeps the process entirely within the digital domain from start to finish. That's a highly efficient way to make music, and it gives computers tremendous advantages, both sonically and ergonomically.

It helps to understand just how audio is recorded digitally, regardless of the technology at hand, before dealing with the tools that aid in that process. Following is a brief rundown on the five key steps in turning a musical idea into a finished CD.

Recording

To most people the word "recording" refers to the entire process of storing music on a machine. But to recordists, *recording* is specific to the initial capturing of the musical performance onto disk. In the lingo of recordists and musicians, *tracking* is used synonymously with recording, because it also refers to the *laying down* of a musical performance to a *track*—once a linear channel on a tape and now a convenient metaphor for hard disk–based recording.

Recording is where you sing into a microphone and where instrumentalists all assemble in a room and bang, blow, or scrape on their respective instruments. It's the part of the process that involves the musicians and their performances, and it's arguably the most critical situation musically and artistically, because that's the stage where the performances occur. But for the recordists, it's only the beginning.

In theory, if the musicians perform perfectly and nothing goes wrong, all that's left to do is stamp the CD. Fortunately for us recordists, this is seldom the case, and we get to tinker with all sorts of aspects of the performance along the way to the master product. Figure 1-2 shows the signal path in the initial recording stage.

Figure 1-2
The elements in the initial recording (or tracking) stage

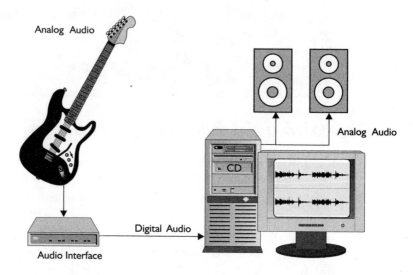

A subset of recording is *overdubbing,* the overlaying of additional musical material after the initial musical elements have been laid down. Overdubbing involves musicians listening back to the previously recorded material and contributing new parts—such as harmony vocals, instrumental fills between sections, and added instruments to bolster the originals.

It is overdubbing that allows artists such as Stevie Wonder to play all the instruments on his albums. He can't play keyboards and the harmonica simultaneously, but he can do the next best thing: play and record the keyboards first, listen back to the track, and play the harmonica along in perfect synchronization with the keyboard part. He and other musicians can do this by using a special machine called a *multitrack tape recorder*. And now the computer can act as a multitrack as easily as it can a flight simulator or word processor.

Editing

After recording the music, the next step is editing. This is the stage where you as a recording specialist go back and examine the musical performances for their quality and make adjustments to the sound.

Small-scale editing (or micro-editing) involves correcting bad notes, deleting noises (such as a breath or lip smack before a vocal entrance), and other spot fixes. Large-scale editing can involve copying whole sections of music (such as the song's chorus) and pasting them in different places of the song. In this way, editing music is like word processing. The digital aspect of music makes it very easy to cut up into its various discrete components and reorder them with seamless results. Figure 1-3 shows small-scale editing of a waveform on a popular digital two-track audio recorder, Steinberg's WaveLab.

Figure 1-3
WaveLab's editing screen shows audio editing on the micro, or waveform, level.

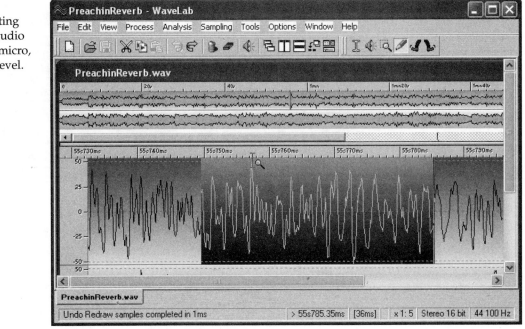

Mixing

Mixing is the process of taking all the separately recorded tracks in a multitrack project and blending them together in the desired balance of volume and stereo positioning. Mixing is also where you add effects, such as reverb and equalization (EQ), to your sound. In analog times, the mixdown deck was separate from the multitrack deck, so it was obvious that these two tasks were separate. In digital times, you're not only using the same machine to do both, you're using the same piece of software. So it helps to remember that the processes are different enough to be considered as separate artistic tasks.

Figure 1-4 shows the mixer window of Steinberg's Cubase SX. The interface features virtual sliders and knobs, laid out much the same as they would be on a large hardware-based tabletop model.

Figure 1-4
The mixer window of Cubase SX sports virtual faders, switches, and knobs, just like its tabletop counterparts.

Mixing is still a stage that one goes through even if there are not multiple tracks to blend. For example, if you're recording a vocalist singing an unaccompanied melody, you might wonder what there is to "mix" after the original recording. Even if everything is perfect from a performance perspective, chances are there's still some global control you'd like to make before sending the initial recording to CD. Most likely, you'd want to add some sort of effect, such as reverb, EQ, or compression (level control). Many people avoid putting effects (especially reverb) at the tracking stage because they prefer to leave the raw track untouched and record effects at the mixdown stage. If you record reverb at the tracking stage, you won't be able to separate it out later on. But if you wait until mixdown, you can experiment with different amounts and types of effects without permanently altering the original.

A lot of people think that whereas tracking is merely getting the sound onto disk accurately and with no mistakes, mixing is an art form. Tracking can be workmanlike, and mixing allows you to show a little flair, but both are equally important in producing a successful end product.

Mastering

Mastering has twin meanings in recording. It can refer to the process after mixing, where further tweaks are made to the finished mixdowns, and it can sometimes mean the process of making the master CD itself. For our purposes, we'll leave the creation of the CD to the *burning* stage and use *mastering* to denote the process of smoothing out the mixed tracks.

Even after a careful mixdown, you can listen to individual mixes of separate songs and sometimes hear disparities. Song 1 might sound louder than Song 2, or the bass on two different songs with similar instrumentation might sound drastically inconsistent from a tonal perspective. Mastering is the process that takes into account and deals with these issues, and it gives your recordings an overall professional sheen and consistency. Mastering is particularly important in creating an album, suite, or any collection of material where you want to preserve a continuity of sound between songs as well as within individual songs.

Burning

This is the simplest and most intuitive of all the processes in the recording chain. It's the part where you take your finished work (in the form of a stereo digital file) and transfer it to a CD. It's called *burning* because you're actually using the drive mechanism's laser beam to etch data (pits) permanently into the compact disc medium. Virtually all new computers come built with a CD-burning drive, and it's a simple matter of using software to operate it. Of course, you need to supply the blank CDs, but these are sold everywhere, including pharmacies and record stores. Current prices of blank CD-Rs (the write-once variety) are less than a dollar apiece (cheaper if you buy in bulk and at discount sources), so they're cheaper than cassette tapes (remember those?).

Burning completes the process of start-to-finish music production on the PC. When you consider that you can take your most fleeting musical impulses—an idea for a melody, a synth texture, a percussion loop—and draw it, play it, or import it into the computer, and then, several steps later, burn it onto a disc that plays in your car, your DiscMan, or your brother-in-law's boom box, that's pretty impressive. And it's not only possible, it's actually easy.

Separating the Hard from the Soft

When all is right with the world, your computer and any attendant gear will act as one system, perfectly functioning as a unit and humming along happily. When you do need to break the system down to its component parts, such as when there's a problem or when you want to upgrade, it helps to divide the system into two big divisions: hardware and software. Both must work in harmony, but each is separate.

Hardware

The hardware of your system is the physical part you can touch—the computer and its circuitry, and any peripherals you've attached to it with cords. Once hardware is installed, it's largely a "set and forget" operation. You can usually change any hardware device's settings with a software control (e.g., from a choice in a drop-down menu), and it's rare that you'll need to, for example, open up the computer's case to make an adjustment on a card or chip. There's no greater feeling than to install a chip or card inside the computer's case and see it represented as a new menu item in your favorite software program.

Hardware for the computer-music recordist can be broken down into three categories: the computer itself, the computer's external peripherals, and your outboard audio peripherals. When you want to purchase a computer, you need to be aware of its internal configuration—what kind of processor it has, what the size and speed of the hard drive is, how much RAM is included. That's the part you can't see, but it defines the computer at its most elemental level.

External peripherals include monitors, keyboards, and mice—things you'd need to operate the computer normally, but the choice of which might be influenced by your music-making activities. Audio-based peripherals (discussed in detail in Chapter 2) include specific devices that connect to your computer for music. These include interfaces (boxes that convert microphone and instrument signals into digital audio), controllers (devices that give you better control than your mouse or keyboard would for making onscreen changes), and other gizmos that perhaps aren't essential to running the computer but may be important or indispensable for music-making.

Table 1-1 lists the typical discount or "street" prices for the most common peripherals. Note that these are estimated prices in U.S. dollars and reflect current pricing at the time this book went to press.

Computer Peripheral	Enhanced for Music	Price	Notes
Monitor	Flat-panel display	$300 for 15"	Because you'll have other gear crowding your workspace, a flat-panel screen will give you more room to put other items at your fingertips or tucked behind the monitor.
Mouse	Programmable wheel mouse	$30–$50	A wheel mouse allows you to scroll through parameters or adjust values by turning a little wheel rather than dragging a scroll bar. Mac users should opt for a two-button mouse.
Keyboard	Standard version okay	$15–$40	
Scanner	Standard version okay	$50–$130	Some software programs allow you to scan in sheet music and convert it to MIDI files.
Printer	Standard version okay	$100–$250	
USB hub	Standard version okay	$30–$40	A hub is a box that allows multiple USB (Universal Serial Bus) devices to connect to the computer via one cable.
FireWire card	Standard version okay	$50–$75	Video cameras and some interfaces use FireWire instead of USB.
Speakers	High-quality speakers with subwoofer	$100–$1,500	It's best to go with true reference monitors than the multimedia speakers included with computer purchases. But if you must go with the latter, get a system with a separate low-frequency subwoofer.

Table 1-1
Discount Prices for Common Peripherals

Computer Peripheral	Enhanced for Music	Price	Notes
Ethernet card (if not already built in)	Standard version okay	$50	Some recording devices are making use of Ethernet as a way of transferring data, so an Ethernet card is a good thing to have.
Internal CD drive	CD-RW drive or better	$120–$300	CD-ROM drives are still available on budget models, but opt for a CD-RW or a DVD-RAM drive, because it will allow you to burn audio CDs right from your computer.
External drive	Standard version okay	$250	Because audio requires a lot of memory, it's best to go with an external SCSI, USB, or FireWire hard drive, but even a 100MB Zip disk can hold nine minutes of CD-quality stereo material. If your computer doesn't have an internal CD-RW drive, get one because it will serve double-duty as a backup drive and CD burner.

Table 1-1
Discount Prices for Common Peripherals *(continued)*

Software

Software is the part of the computer that people are most familiar with, because it interacts with the user directly through its screen, keyboard, and mouse inter-faces. Software includes applications (also called *programs),* files (the things you create using applications, also called *documents),* drivers (special, non-user-al-terable files used to help software talk to hardware), and the operating system (the underlying platform over which all applications run). When you start up your computer to write a letter, you launch a word processing application, create a file (after you name and save your work), and then work on your letter until it's perfected—creating new text, editing entered text, formatting, tweaking. Then you might print a hard copy version or e-mail your file as an attachment.

The musical process works the same way, except that instead of typing, you're playing an instrument or singing into the computer as your way of input-ting data. Software is the means for creating and shaping your creative work, and its interface (the onscreen parameters you control) helps you create, edit, and tweak the data that will eventually be output to a CD or a digital file format such as MP3 or WAV (pronounced "wave").

Music software has become highly specialized, and we'll get in depth with the many different types of programs and their uses in Chapter 3. But for now, Table 1-2 will give you a good idea of the range of software that's out there for music production.

Software Type	Uses
Digital audio + MIDI sequencer	Multitrack audio and MIDI recording, composing, and scoring to video.
Two-track audio recorder/editor	For stereo work only or for mastering work after mixing down from multitrack audio/MIDI software.
Software-based samplers, synthesizers, and effects	For replacing the hardware versions of outboard samplers, synth modules, and effects processors by bringing these tasks into the computer's domain and gaining better integration with the host recorder.
MP3, Windows Media Audio, QuickTime, RealAudio encoder/player	For converting WAV and AIFF files into MP3/WMA/QuickTime/RealAudio files (some two-track and audio/sequencer software will do this, too) and for playing back those file formats.
Notation software	For creating printed scores of your work. Some programs convert scanned sheet music into MIDI files.
Calculator	For converting beats per minute into real time, samples into milliseconds, and frequency transpositions into tempo changes as well as for calculating delay times, and so on.
Metronome utility	For simple time-keeping tasks without your having to launch a full-fledged sequencer.
Peer-to-peer file-sharing utility	For finding and downloading MP3 files on the Internet.
CD-burning software	For creating audio and data CDs.
Disk repair/utility	For hard disk repair/maintenance and defragmenting.
Inexpensive video/movie program	For simple video scoring and sound editing within the video environment.

Table I-2
Software for Music Production

How the Different Hardware Components Contribute

Each component in a computer system—whether hardware or software based—has a role to play, and it helps to know what each does before embarking on music production. Let's begin with the physical aspects of the computer, because they're the ones that handle audio on the most basic level: converting it from sounds in the air or along an instrument cable into digital data on your hard drive, just ripe for experimentation.

Interfaces and Converters

In one world you have singing and expression. In the other you have data and editing. How does one world become the other? The answer lies in *hardware interfaces,* boxes that connect musical gear such as microphones, guitars, keyboards, and drum machines to the ports (sockets) on the back of your computer. An interface is simply a go-between that connects one device to another. Because a computer wasn't built expressly to capture your death-metal guitar wailings, you must employ a translator that can convert the language of a wildly thrashing guitar into the ones and zeros that the more button-down computer understands.

A good interface makes operations simple on both sides. A musician should be able to work with it in musical terms when plugging in, and the computer operator should be comfortable with the data integrity of its output. Because these two roles are often played by the same person (namely you), you want a device that's logical, obvious, and reliable no matter which end you're approaching it from. Though it's often possible to plug a mic, guitar, or keyboard directly into a computer's built-in soundcard, this isn't always the best way to get a sound or to take advantage of the software's capability. Interfaces are built to bridge that gap, and they often come with software components that, once installed, allow the application to "see" and configure the interface for optimal operation.

A converter is somewhat like an interface in that it turns one kind of information into another, but it's even more basic because it does only one thing: convert the sound of the analog world around us into the data of the digital world that lives inside the computer and then reconvert the computer-generated digital data back into the analog signals that drive speakers and headphones. Converters are often included in an interface, so you rarely have to think of them separately, but it helps to know that at the very essence of your interface lies the conversion of analog signals into digital data.

Processors

The processor is the first component we'll visit that lurks in the heart of the computer's insides. The computer's processor is the brains of the operation, the most important single component affecting the computer's performance. It includes the chip that performs all the calculations necessary to do everything in recording—from capturing musical performances, to adding reverb, to uploading MP3 files to the Web.

When discussing a computer, it's more meaningful to refer to its processor type and speed rather than its make and model. For example, when people talk of a "two-gig Pentium IV," they're speaking of the processor—the chip that the rest of the components (power supply, RAM, etc.) serve. A Pentium III at 800 MHz is of an older generation and speed than a Pentium IV at 2.0 GHz. As a rule, the newer and faster the processor is, the better. That's true for *all* computing tasks, including music. But it's not a simple matter of just buying the "latest and greatest" (unless you're rich and can afford to turn over your computer every couple of months). You should always have a computer with a reasonably up-to-date processor, but for music, you can often do just fine with last-year's model.

RAM

RAM (Random Access Memory) is the temporary, working memory of a computer, and it has to be large enough to launch the application you're using and to hold the files you've got open. For music production, more RAM means more available tracks to record and play back on and more real-time effects (EQ, reverb, compression) you can have active simultaneously. Like the proverbial adage about being too rich or too thin, you can never have enough RAM—especially in an all-computer environment where you're relying on the computer for effects, which, in a hybrid system of computers and outboard gear, might be handled by external devices.

Hard Drive

The hard drive stores your operating system (which boots up and runs the computer), your applications (the programs you "launch" to begin working), and your files (the work you create and save with the applications). Current computer technology sees hard drives getting larger at a faster rate than software can consume completely the space on them, so for the musician, the prognosis is good: A new computer that comes with at least a 40 GB hard drive is more than enough to run applications and hold a lot of music.

CD Drive

A CD-RW (read/write) drive is absolutely essential for music production, because that's how you will create the final product—a compact disc that will play in any audio CD player. But the drive itself is all the way downstream from the music-making process, and the actual production of the disc takes place after the work is completed and finalized, so it doesn't affect your music directly. You need a CD-RW drive, but it doesn't actually "contribute" to the process the way the other components do. Important specs and other considerations for CD drives are discussed in the section "Minimum Requirements for a Recording PC."

Operating Systems

The operating system is what makes your computer work, telling the chips and other mysterious gizmos inside the box what to do and providing colorful and user-friendly screens on your monitor for you to fill in, rearrange, and otherwise play with. Software applications run on top of the operating system and therefore must be carefully written in conjunction with the OS's specs to take advantages of its features and to avoid illegal operations (which result in crashes). Operating systems are constantly evolving, so applications must be rewritten (along with the applications' own schedule of improvements and bug fixes) to keep current with them.

A major operating system update is front-page news, and its numerical designations are familiar terms to computer consumers. From Microsoft the major releases are Windows 3.1, Windows 95, Windows 98, Windows Me, Windows NT, Windows 2000, and Windows XP. On the Apple Macintosh side, there were generations of Mac OSs (6.x through 9.2) before the completely revamped OS X (pronounced *oh-ess ten*) version 10.2 (Jaguar). There are other operating systems, such as Linux, which is gaining popularity, but this book deals only with Windows- and Mac-based software.

Windows

Microsoft Windows is the most popular operating system in the world and is found on computers manufactured by Compaq, Dell, Gateway, Hewlett-Packard, Sony, Toshiba, and others. It works with a variety of processors, including Pentiums, Athlons, and Celerons, and has the widest variety of software programs available, including those for creating music. It's estimated that of all the computers in the world, over 90 percent of them run the Windows operating system. As of this writing, the current version of Windows is XP, available in the Home or Professional version, and either one is fine for self-contained music production. If you're considering working in a computer network environment or using a multiprocessor machine, XP Professional is recommended.

Mac OS

Running a distant second as far as market share—though its public image belies this fact—is the Mac OS, manufactured by Apple Computer, Inc. The Mac OS is found only on Apple-manufactured Macintosh computers, so the software is written by the same company that makes the hardware. In the computing world as a whole, the Mac is much less popular than Windows, but in music production, the balance is less skewed in the favor of Windows, and the Mac is more of a presence. The Mac OS is neither better nor worse than Windows for music, though the Mac historically has enjoyed favor among high-end audio production facilities. But that distinction is less clear now, due more to Microsoft's improvement rather than any slacking on the Mac side.

Mac vs. PC

The debate regarding "Windows vs. Mac" gets a lot of attention because the two computer platforms are natural business competitors and because users tend to learn and use one and not the other and therefore develop a certain brand loyalty. But as far as music production is concerned, both are virtually equal in power and usability, and many software programs are written *cross-platform,* which means the same program is available for both Windows and Mac (much like Microsoft's business software suite, Office), and files created by one can be opened by the other.

Whether you choose to go with one operating system over the other has more to do with considerations other than the inherent attributes of the actual operating system. For example, if you want to run Cakewalk SONAR, you'll be a Windows user because SONAR isn't available for the Mac OS. On the Mac-only side is a very widely used program called Digital Performer by Mark of the Unicorn, so if you're joining a DP users' group, you'll be working on a Mac.

But it's very hard to argue the benefits of one system over another based solely on the operating system, a fact that becomes increasingly more difficult as time progresses, as each improves on its own design and acquires features previously unique to its rival. And both tend to look more like each other just through a natural evolution of reaching a design ideal.

Something else to consider: A modern computer-based music producer should have a facility with both systems, even if he or she has a preference for or a historical draw to the other. And the more you work with both platforms, the more you learn how to accomplish exactly the same tasks, once you learn each system's respective way of doing things. Many of the so-called differences between the two systems are mythical (e.g., Macs don't have a right-click option—they do) or can easily be resolved through a configuration change or with a simple third-party utility.

Most bi-platform music people acknowledge the distinctions between working with the Mac OS and Windows, but they don't judge, and it gets harder to answer absolute questions such as "Which is better?" Each has its areas of strength, and any computer system can make you tear your hair out on occasion. Be wary of someone who blindly recommends one over the other for sheer technical superiority. Chances are, that person knows only one operating system or has some other axe to grind. The reality is both are great for music, and they're only getting better.

Minimum Requirements for a Recording PC

If you have all the money in the world, simply buy the best computer you can every three months, throw away (or donate) the old one, and skip the rest of this section. But if you're down here on earth with the rest of us mortals, you should be interested in what the minimum requirements are for music production in a computer so that you're not spending $2,000 more than you have to, if you just want to sing your songs and play your acoustic guitar into the computer. Recording music requires some power—more than word processing, but less than video production. But how much power you need, and therefore how much money you need to spend, can be a tricky issue because music software's needs change as the hardware evolves, making the selection of a system a moving-target proposition.

This section details the primary components of the computer and what are considered minimum requirements for professional music production in a new computer, assuming you'll be running Windows XP or Mac OS X.

Processor

Windows machines use processors named Pentium (manufactured by Intel), Celeron (also by Intel), and Athlon (by AMD). If you're looking to buy a new computer for music, I recommend either a Pentium or Athlon with a speed of at least 1 GHz (*gigahertz*, or one billion cycles per second; 1 GHz = 1,000 MHz). However, you can do minimal music production with a Celeron-configured machine or with boxes that have slower processors, as long as you don't go below 300 MHz. If you must make do with the bare-bones approach (such as a 200 MHz PII, a perfectly good machine), check the software that you'll be running to make sure it will work.

On the Mac side, the processors are named for the model, so a G3 computer has a G3 processor, and a G4 computer has a G4 processor. The speed of these two processors ranges from about 300 MHz to over 2 GHz, but a G3 "blue & white" (as opposed to "beige") 400 MHz processor would be the minimum. Again, a good way to know exactly "how low you can go" (as they say when dancing the limbo) is to simply check the minimum system requirements of the specific software you plan to use. They're often conveniently labeled "Minimum System Requirements," and many manufacturers distinguish between minimum and recommended. As a poor but earnest musician, I've found I have recommended tastes but minimum finances.

RAM

Most budget systems come outfitted with 128MB of RAM, but the recommended minimum for music is 256MB. So either choose the manufacturer's offer of upgrading to at least 256MB or consider buying additional RAM from a third party and installing it yourself. RAM prices fluctuate, so seek advice and check prices about when the right time to upgrade your RAM is. For example, at the time of this writing, RAM is a steal—about $25 for 256MB, even cheaper with rebate programs.

Hard Drive(s)

The hard drive that comes with a new computer will be enough for you to launch your software and create quite a bit of music before you have storage concerns. This technology sees larger and larger hard drives coming out at cheaper and cheaper prices, whereas software's appetites to consume those gigabytes grow at a slower rate, so musicians can set up shop and get to work without thinking about outgrowing their new system—for a little while, anyway.

Stereo audio takes up about 10MB per minute, so an 80GB hard drive—assuming you leave aside about 10GB for the operating system and applications—will hold about 70GB or 7,000 minutes (116 hours) of stereo audio, or over 875 minutes (14.5 hours) of 16-track audio projects. That's pretty roomy, for audio purposes. If you were a video producer, that wouldn't last you until lunch.

A hard drive for music production must not only be capacious but have a fast spindle rate (measured in revolutions per minute, or *rpm*) and a fast seek time (the time it takes for the drive to read the data off of the spinning platter, measured in milliseconds, or *ms*). A rate of 7200 rpm is recommended for music production, though you can get away with the slower speed of 5400 rpm found on older machines, especially if you're not trying to keep more than four or eight tracks going. Times in the teens (e.g., 15 ms) are fine for getting data onto and off the drive quickly enough to keep time with the music.

CD Burner

Older computers have read-only CD drives, meaning you can't *create* CDs from them but rather only read and import (transfer data). If you're buying new, don't even think of a system without a CD-RW drive. If you find yourself inheriting granny's CD read-only machine, you'll have to acquire an external CD burner, but you can still use its existing CD-ROM drive for importing loops, samples, and other musical bits that come from audio and data CDs.

For modern CD drives, you have a choice of CD-RW or the more expensive DVD burners (also called DVD-RAM drives), which include the ability to burn in the CD-R and CD-RW formats. CD-RW drives' specs are often listed as three numbers separated by slashes, as in 24/10/40. Here's how to read that notation: The CD-R rate (burning a write-once CD) is at 24× (24 times speed), the CD-RW rate (burning a rewriteable CD) is at 10×, and the CD read rate is at 40×. The recording speed of a CD is how long it takes to burn your data. To burn a 650MB CD-R, which holds 74 minutes of music, requires 74 minutes at 1×. At 24×, you can burn the same amount of music in three minutes. In reality, it takes a little longer, because you have to add some time on either end for the burner to format the CD with its lead-in and lead-out data, but the faster the CD mechanism, the less time you'll spend staring at the onscreen taskbar while making copies of your music for your family and friends.

Ports

Ports are the holes, or sockets, in your computer that allow you attach devices to it. You're probably already familiar with the ports you have that allow you to hook up your monitor, keyboard, mouse, and printer—a computer must be able to accommodate these basic devices, or it wouldn't be much good for real-world use. But the well-configured music computer includes extra ports of the same variety or different ones that should be considered as minimum for music production.

USB

USB (Universal Serial Bus) is the newer protocol for attaching mice, keyboards, printers, scanners, and other common computer devices, but many MIDI and audio interfaces use USB as well, so look for a computer that has at least two USB ports. You can buy an external USB hub, which allows you to plug multiple devices into the hub, and then run a single cable from the hub to just one of the computer's USB ports. When you consider that you'll probably have a printer, a keyboard, an audio or MIDI interface, a scanner, and a Zip drive all vying for USB attention, a hub may become a necessity, so be sure to factor it into your budget.

PCI Slots

In a desktop or tower computer, the back panel has several slots, usually covered with metal plates, that designate the PCI (Peripheral Computer Interconnect) slots. Many add-ons and peripherals require a PCI slot for installation, such as soundcards, multichannel audio interfaces, and video and monitor cards. The cards go inside the computer's case, snapped into special cradles, and their particular sockets (9-pin, RCA, 5-pin MIDI, Toslink optical, 1/4" phone, etc.) stick out of the back of the computer's case slightly, allowing you to plug in external devices. Most computers come with three or more PCI slots (the G4 iMac is an exception in that it has none), but depending on the configuration (what peripherals are included with the system), one or more of these slots may already be occupied (e.g., by a monitor card). Figure 1-5 shows a view of the computer's back-panel PCI slots and a typical card inserted into one of them.

Figure I-5
The back panel of a tower computer, showing three PCI slots, the bottom one occupied by a soundcard sporting a 25-pin DIN port (with a trapezoid shape) plus two RCA (or coaxial) digital S/PDIF jacks

PCMCIA

PCMCIA (Personal Computer Memory Card International Association) is the laptop computer's high-speed data-throughput answer to the desktop's PCI slot. One of the PCMCIA slot's more common uses is for hooking up a network card, but in music and audio applications, manufacturers will often make interfaces that connect through a card that plugs into this slot. All laptop computers include a PCMCIA slot, so it's not something you have to watch out for, as far as its inclusion, but you should know that it's capable of being pressed into recording service. You can even buy adapters that will bridge a PCI chassis to a PCMCIA slot for using PCI cards with laptops. Figure 1-6 shows the Digigram Vxpocket, a powerful system for bringing lots of signals in and out of a laptop from its unassuming PCMCIA interface.

Figure 1-6
A laptop can
now get in on
the audio action
with a PCMCIA
interface—its
version of the
desktop's
PCI slot.

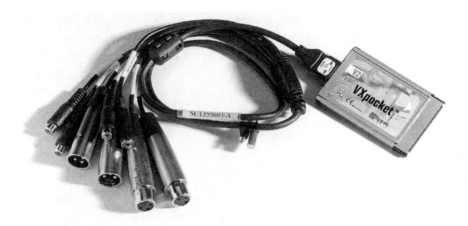

FireWire (IEEE 1394)

The high-speed communications protocol, officially called IEEE 1394 but known better by the colloquial "FireWire," is used with digital video cameras and is becoming more and more popular as a means for transferring audio into and out of the computer. It's not essential to have a FireWire port on your computer unless you're considering a FireWire device, such as a controller/interface such as Mark of the Unicorn's 828 or 896, or Digidesign's 002.

As far as usability, FireWire is like USB: it's hot-swappable (meaning you don't have to turn off the computer to plug your devices in and pull them out for safe, reliable operation), it's found on both laptops and desktops, and the wires are *directional,* with different shaped plugs at either end. But FireWire is so much faster than USB version 1.1 that it can be used to transfer high-resolution audio (with specs much higher than CD audio) and multichannel audio (good for recording multiple tracks simultaneously). However, with the introduction of USB 2 and FireWire 2, the differences between the two protocols will be less drastic. At current writing, FireWire is a common solution for more professional systems. Plus, FireWire is found on both laptops and desktops, so if you're thinking of having a portable as well as stationary setup, a FireWire interface is the way to go, until USB 2 catches up.

Computer Peripherals

For music, you don't need a special mouse or keyboard, as discussed earlier in "Separating the Hard from the Soft." All music software programs are designed to work with the standard-issue models of these familiar input devices. There are just a couple items that don't strictly make music but become greatly useful for music-making activities and should be considered when creating a recommended setup.

External Disk Drives

An external disk drive is highly recommended for music-making, because it's just reckless to spend hours and hours creating music files and then not having a responsible backup solution at hand. You can't back up music files on a floppy disk (floppy drives come built in to most Windows-configured machines) because the files are too big. A second, internal hard drive is a good thing to have, because it allows you to keep your operating system and applications on one drive, and your files on the other. But if you can have only one additional drive, other than the primary hard drive that houses your operating system and applications, it should be external.

The advantage of being external is that the disk sits physically away from the computer and can be easily moved and hooked up to another computer (such as your laptop) in case either the primary computer or its boot disk fail. Also, keeping backup files in separate locations is good in case of a physical catastrophe, such as an anvil dropping on one of them, or an accidental misfire from a Klingon taser. In really critical projects, you can take the external drive away with you and lock it in a vault or place it under your pillow for the ultimate in safekeeping. Prices are coming down all the time, but at this writing, an 80GB external FireWire drive costs about $175, and USB drives are even cheaper.

Second Monitor and Video Monitor Cards

Not a minimum requirement, but certainly worth considering, is a large monitor with its own PCI video card. Music involves recording, editing, and mixing, and they're all performed using different windows in your software. It's nice not to have to shuffle your screens around like a game of Three-Card Monty, and a large monitor of 17" or more will let you keep open and view more windows simultaneously.

A large screen requires power, though, and a video PCI card helps drive the monitor so that it doesn't tax the system, causing slow redraws and unstable performance in the critical audio functions. Consider a video card with at least 16MB, and make sure you have an available PCI slot if you decide on a new monitor.

Having two monitors is a great benefit when working with audio. For many computer-based activities, one monitor is fine. It's hard to imagine needing more than one screen to write a letter or to browse the Web. But in music, you often want to refer to several windows simultaneously, to check different aspects of a musical performance. For example, as the music plays back, you might want to view the overall arrangement as it proceeds through the verses and choruses, but you might want to also view the faders' movement in the mixer window. In a large project of 16 tracks or more, you can't fit more than one window on the screen, even on a 17" monitor. But with two side-by-side monitors, you can arrange multiple windows across the two screens.

To run two monitors, though, you'll need to add at least one PCI card, or perhaps one card with two outputs. At this writing, you can buy a 17" monitor with its own card for about $110. Flat-panel displays are more desirable, but they're more expensive. You can get a 15" display for just under $300, but prices are going down all the time and may be competitive enough with the CRT (cathode ray tube)—the heavier, bulkier picture-tube models we're all familiar with—that you may decide it's worth it to go with a flat panel for its convenience and space-saving advantages.

Configuring Your System à la Carte

Due to a computer's modular nature, you always have some choices to make when buying a system from a manufacturer or retailer. At the very least, you can choose one monitor over another, or a multibutton optical mouse over the standard issue that comes at no additional charge. But especially in the Windows world, you can often dictate which key components you'd like, getting this type of processor, that type of hard drive, this amount of RAM, and so on.

You can get a good feel for this process by visiting Dell Computer's Web site (www.dell.com) and clicking through to their refurbished systems page. Here, through pull-down menus, you can select from every category exactly which component you want in your system. This allows you to see whether it's any cheaper to go with a 1.8 GHz Pentium processor and a 40GB hard drive or with a 2.0 GHz Celeron processor and a 30GB hard drive. A manufacturer may not have systems available in all configurations, but you can at least get an idea for the process. Figure 1-7 shows how you can custom-tailor your own system.

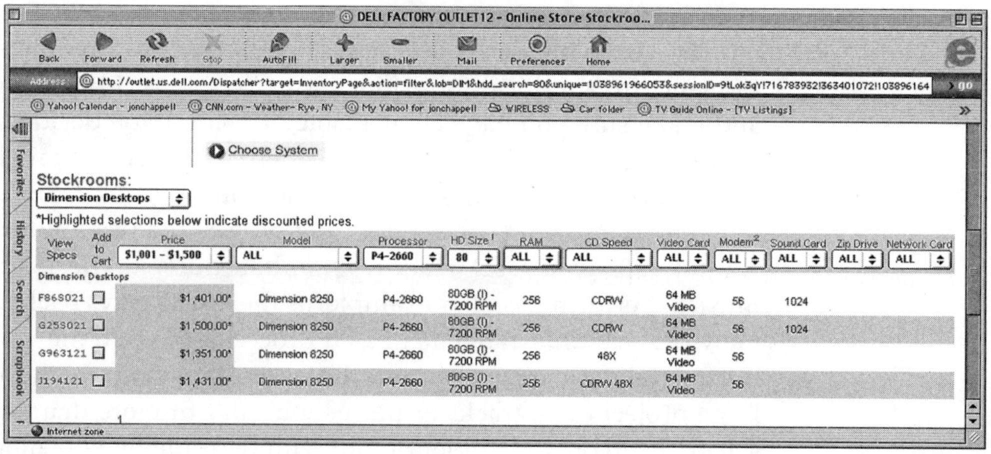

Figure I-7
The pull-down menus show choices made for price ($1,000–$1,500), processor type (Pentium 4/2600), and hard drive size (80MB), but unselected menus have allowed for all the possibilities of other components, such as RAM, CD speed, video card, and so on.

Turnkey Solutions

In the interest of granting equal time, I'll mention turnkey systems, a phrase that describes a preconfigured system expressly designed for some specialized musical purpose. A turnkey system is configured "à la carte," usually by an audio specialist who knows which components from all the myriad of available ones are best for your situation. Do you know the make and model of the quietest yet most powerful fan for a given motherboard and case? A turnkey specialist does. Ditto for power supplies, processors, RAM, hard drives, and so on.

But perhaps just as important as the turnkey specialist's knowledge is his commitment to technical support. The biggest problem in building a system—that is, choosing hardware and software components that may never have been tested to work with one another—is that conflicts, gremlins, and other productivity-sapping evils can, and will, arise. Tech support is worth its weight in gold when you get stuck with a system breakdown at deadline time, and an angel of mercy—one who knows music and audio and not just the nuts and bolts of computers—appears. You'll be glad to have paid for the service.

The turnkey system comes with a desirable extra: a human. But generally, you can build your own system without a specialist, and if problems arise, solving them yourself teaches you a little something more about your system—and possibly anger management.

Laptops

Special mention must be made for the case of laptop computers and audio, as their star has risen lately as viable music-making computers. It used to be that laptops, although equal to their desktop counterparts in computing tasks such as word processing and business applications, were unsuited to music, because their physical configuration prevented connecting PCI devices—the connection method of choice for many popular audio and music interfaces. But since the rise of USB and FireWire in audio hardware (whose small ports fit just as well on a laptop as a desktop), laptop computers have become contenders as serious recording machines. Another improvement in laptops is hard drive speeds. In the past, laptops might have had processors that were as fast as their desktop counterparts, but their hard drive mechanisms were not as fast. But that, too, is now being addressed, and many people cotton to the idea of using a laptop to record a symphony orchestra, an 18-piece big band, or a Grateful Dead–style cluster jam.

Oh, and about the reduced monitor, cramped keyboard, and that pencil eraser they call a mouse? You can always hook up a full-size 19" monitor, an extended ergonomically curved keyboard, and your favorite cordless optical mouse through the laptop's onboard video and USB ports.

Moving On

Now that you have an idea of the basic computer components and how they relate to music production, let's remain in the physical world (i.e., dealing with stuff you can touch) but look at some other types of peripherals for capturing musical sounds and getting them ready for the journey through the wonderful world of computers. Chapter 2 explores the music-hardware peripherals that will help you convert all your recording impulses into computer commands, allowing you to keep your soul as a musician while speaking computerese to that unassuming box on your desk with no visible moving parts.

Chapter 2
Music and Audio Peripherals

In Chapter 1 we looked at the computer itself and the peripherals that make general computer-based work easier and more efficient. Now we'll look at peripherals of a different sort: those specific to music and audio production.

The hardware category that bridges the world of music-making with the world of digital storage and manipulation is referred to as *peripherals*, but these are the peripherals that distinguish the way a musical person versus, say, an accountant approaches a computer. A healthy computer functions much the same way internally when applying reverb to a vocal track as it does when crunching spreadsheet formulas, but it's the critical difference of *inputting* and *translating* the music into data that distinguishes an audio production setup from a business one, at least as far as the hardware is concerned.

The first step is to create a good musical sound—whether that's screaming rock-and-roll guitar riffs, the lilting arpeggios of an Irish harp, or the soulful vocal harmonies of a gospel choir. After achieving a good sound, the next step is to put it all on a wire. Even before we approach our desktop box, the music must be in electrical form, whether it's from a microphone, a mixer, or the output jack of the instrument itself. Then the fun begins, because, fortunately for us musical types, there are scores of devices that make music-making on a computer more like a job for a musician than a geek in a white lab coat.

Better Living Through Music and Audio Peripherals

The traditional computer user has two primary tools for controlling the computer at his disposal: the mouse and the keyboard. Neither one was designed for making music. Worse, neither was designed for controlling the music after it has been captured onto disk, either. If you look at your stereo system, or a guitar amplifier, or an electronic keyboard, you won't see a mouse or an alphanumeric keyboard anywhere. So armies of clever hardware designers created musical tools that bridge that gap. The first step in the computer-music chain doesn't look much different from what you'd take to a garage-band jam: your musical instrument. In computer lingo, it's called the *input device.*

Choose Your Weapon: Input Devices

In order to record music onto a computer, it would be useful to be able to make music in the first place. You can get data into a computer in a variety of ways, but because we're talking about music, let's examine how you would use a musical instrument as an input device, even if that is a funny name to describe an eighteenth-century Stradivarius. A computer doesn't judge your musical talents or tastes, or the aesthetic quality of an audio signal. It doesn't care what style or genre that signal is (in fact, it doesn't even care if it's music at all, in the traditional sense), as long as it meets certain electrical requirements. For the moment, we'll treat music, the artistic stuff, as *audio*, the language you need to speak to a computer.

Microphones

The most familiar input device is the *microphone.* A mic ("mike") is like an electronic ear in that it hears what you hear, assuming you're standing in the same vicinity. Its diaphragm and capsule convert acoustic energy (sound) to electrical energy (current), which is sent along a wire. A mic is what you use to record a singer, a pianist, or any other source that produces acoustic sound, including an electric guitar coming out of the speaker of an amplifier.

A mic works intuitively: Put it close to the source, and the recorded sound will sound close up; put it further from the source, and the sound will sound further away, possessing an ambient quality. The one disadvantage to a mic is that because its sound-generating elements are so sensitive to acoustic impulses, the electrical current it produces is very weak. Therefore, it must be boosted by a preamp, and that necessitates using a separate box for best results. Preamps are included on some soundcards, but the best preamps exist as external boxes—an additional peripheral.

Microphones come in two basic types: dynamic and condenser. A dynamic mic doesn't require external power to work; you just plug it into your soundcard, preamp, or mixer, and start passing audio. Dynamics are good for really loud signals—such as cranked up guitar amps or bass drums—and they're ideal for stage performance, but they're not the best choice for all-around recording work. For vocals, acoustic instruments, and other general-purpose studio work, a condenser mic will yield the best results in terms of *frequency response* (high highs and low lows) and *sensitivity* (details of the sound). A condenser mic requires external power, called *phantom power,* to work, and that's supplied by circuitry in a preamp or other device. That means you can't plug a condenser mic directly into a soundcard, but the extra gizmo you need to drive a condenser mic is worth it for the quality improvement over dynamics that these mics provide.

In recent years, the price of quality condenser mics has dropped, and manufacturers have gotten quite competitive in delivering many and varied affordable condenser mics to home recordists on a budget. Large-diaphragm condensers are considered the best all-around choice for a mic, if it's your first, or if you can only have one. Companies such as AKG, Audio-Technica, M-Audio, Marshall Electronics, and Shure all offer a wide range of excellent large-diaphragm mics at affordable prices. Figure 2-1 shows the AKG C414, a popular large-diaphragm mic seated in its *shock mount* (a suspension system that disconnects the mic from the stand) on a mic stand *boom* (a horizontal arm that allows greater positioning flexibility).

Figure 2-1
A large-diaphragm condenser mic, such as the AKG C414, is suitable for many recording uses, including vocals, acoustic instruments, electric guitars, and drums.

Keyboards

An electronic keyboard has an advantage over a microphone in that the signal it produces doesn't need a preamp, so you can plug the keyboard directly into the computer without an intermediary device. You'll still need to hear what you're playing, and for that you can use a keyboard amplifier, headphones, or the computer's speakers—but at least electrically speaking, the output of a keyboard can talk directly to a computer's soundcard or other interface (explained later), assuming the cord's plug correctly fits the interface's jack.

A keyboard is a good master input device to have in your studio, even if it's not your main performing instrument. When you want to input general music information into your computer, regardless of whether it's actually a piano, organ, or other keyboard-based instrument, an electronic keyboard is often the best tool for the job. Figure 2-2 shows the Roland Fantom, a full-featured workstation keyboard that has onboard sampling, synthesis, and MIDI sequencing capabilities. This type of keyboard provides an excellent source for rich, synthesized sounds and realistic samples of acoustic and orchestral instruments.

Figure 2-2
The Roland Fantom is a pro-level keyboard that has many features suited for digital recording, including synthesis, sampling, and MIDI sequencing.

Drum Machines

A drum machine is something most computer-based musicians eventually come to own because it produces *sampled* (digitally recorded) drum sounds that can be played and programmed into patterns and grooves—from single instruments, such as a conga or clavé, to a full drum kit. A drum machine not only has drum sounds but also pads with which to play the drum sounds, making it a better device for pounding out drum parts than, say, a guitar or keyboard. If you can't play drum parts yourself, a drum machine also has an onboard *sequencer* (pattern composer) that allows you to create your own groove right within the machine, though it's often preferable to create the drum patterns on the computer software and use the drum machine in slave (sound output–only) mode. Figure 2-3 shows a popular, mid-level drum machine, the Boss DR-770, which provides lots of traditional and ethnic percussion samples, powerful control over the sounds' pitch, decay, and pan (position in the stereo field), an onboard sequencer, and pads that allow you to whack out the sounds live.

Figure 2-3
The Boss DR-770 has a wide variety of sounds, a pattern sequencer, and pads that can be struck by the performer.

Electrically, a drum machine's output is similar to an electronic keyboard's and therefore can be plugged directly into the computer's interface without the aid of a preamp. You use the same kind of cable to hook up a drum machine as you do a keyboard or guitar. Having said all this, you don't need a drum machine to add drum parts to your compositions. By importing preexisting grooves and patterns from CDs or by assembling drum hits from samples on your hard disk, you can create drum patterns without any drum machine at all. You can also use the preset drum sounds in a keyboard workstation or synth module. But as an input device, a drum machine is a handy thing to have around.

Electric Guitars

You would think an electric guitar could plug directly into a computer soundcard or interface in the same way keyboards and drum machines do, but it's not advisable for a couple reasons. First, even though the output of an electric guitar is, obviously, electronic and exits the instrument though a cord, the signal is much weaker compared to other electronic instruments. This is due to the guitar's pickups—the guitar's sound-producing devices that give the electric guitar its charm. However, they're just magnets and are fairly weak as far as generating a healthy electronic signal.

The second reason against plugging in directly is that an electric guitar uses the amplifier to help create the special character of its sound. Whereas a keyboardist uses an amp to simply magnify, without distortion, whatever was there in the first place, guitarists use their amps to provide the sound quality or color. An unadorned guitar sound, without the contribution of a guitar amp, is not a terribly useful sound from a musical perspective.

Fortunately for guitarists, there are many fun and cool ways to fix this. The simplest and purest way to capture an electric guitar through a cranked amplifier—the way nature intended—is to stick a mic in front of the amp. Hearing an electric guitar through a speaker is the way you experience it naturally (unlike, say, an acoustic guitar or flute, which doesn't require an amp to produce its core sound). And that's still the best method, and the way big-budget rock albums are produced.

Another approach is to take a signal out of the guitar's amp through the line-out jack in the back of the amp's control panel. This way, the sound gets processed by the amplifier circuitry and gets enough juice behind it to provide the interface with a strong signal. Usually, you can turn down the speaker's volume independently of the line-out jack's level, or even defeat the speaker sound entirely, similar to the way plugging in headphones works. The disadvantage to the line-out method is that you're not getting the effect of the speaker, which many tone snobs agree is integral to the electric guitar's sound.

The third way to capture a guitar sound is to introduce a device that not only brings the guitar signal up to snuff electronically but also simulates what happens to it on its journey through a guitar amp—including the much-sought-after speaker effect. A whole cottage industry has sprung up around boxes designed for recording guitars. The Line 6 POD creates great distortion sounds but also simulates different types of clean signals. Many of the POD's sounds are digitally modeled after famous amps (by Marshall, Fender, Mesa/Boogie, etc.). You can dial up any amp sound you like on the box, plus add other effects such as reverb, chorus, and delay. Figure 2-4 shows the Line 6 POD*XT*, a direct-recording device for plugging a guitar into a computer.

Figure 2-4
The Line 6 POD*XT* is designed to prepare a guitar signal for recording directly into a computer, providing a realistic amp sound, plus effects such as overdrive, reverb, and many others. Simply plug your guitar into the device and attach another cord from the device's output to the computer.

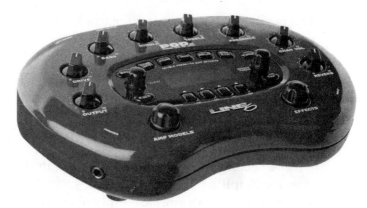

MIDI Input

So far we've talked about instruments as they're played and heard in the traditional way—as audio going into a recording device. But while a keyboard and drum machine are creating sounds through their audio outputs, they're also transmitting another type of data as you play them: MIDI. MIDI stands for Musical Instrument Digital Interface and is the musical language that transmits performance information such as pitch (A, B, C#, etc.), timing (how fast you play the notes in time), and dynamics (how loud or soft you play). No sound is actually transmitted in MIDI, but recording your MIDI performance is a powerful way to create music, especially if you work with electronic instruments (synthesizers, grooveboxes, samplers) and like to compose and edit in a modular style. MIDI is essential in groove-based music, and it's extremely useful for creating songs with well-defined groove and accompaniment approaches (dance, rock, techno, drum'n'bass, etc.).

All drum machines and keyboards have built-in MIDI circuitry and jacks, and they transmit MIDI data right along with the audio signal they output, except that MIDI and audio travel on separate cables that you have to hook up individually.

If you want to create a synthesizer line, you can approach it in two ways: You could record the audio in the normal fashion. But you could also ignore the audio for the moment (except for listening purposes) and record the MIDI data emanating from the synth's MIDI out jack. When you're ready to play back the MIDI data from the computer, you simply hook up a cable from the computer to the keyboard's MIDI in jack and hit "play" on the computer. The computer now "plays" the synthesizer exactly as you had recorded the passage only moments before (mistakes and all!). The only difference is that the keys don't move, but sonically, the keyboard's internal sounds, as played by MIDI, are exactly the same as when you played the keys.

So what's the big deal of this method? Why not just record the audio in the first place and be done with it? The answer lies in how you can change the data once it's recorded. Because you're only recording *performance* information, you can, say, switch the sound on the keyboard from a synth to a flute on playback, and the performance will remain intact and unaffected. You can view the MIDI data onscreen in a format that's much easier and smoother to edit than audio waveforms. Unlike audio, which is represented on a computer as a continuous waveform, MIDI is separated into discrete events and is very easy to manipulate.

Music production with MIDI is analogous to text creation using a typewriter versus a word processor. If you type on a manual typewriter, you produce a direct document on paper. You can edit it, but it's tricky: To change anything, you need Wite-Out, scissors and glue, and additional typed passages on paper if you want to, say, vary the type size and style. But if you enter the words in a word processor first, you can cut, copy, paste, and change the font all very easily before outputting. That's how easy it is to work with MIDI. It responds very well to editing on the micro and large-scale levels.

We'll explore MIDI in more depth in Chapter 4, but right now it's important to understand how useful MIDI capability is in an input device. If you're a guitar player—or an instrumentalist whose instrument doesn't naturally accommodate MIDI, as keyboards do—you can fit a special pickup that converts your particular instrument's audio output to MIDI. Or you can see if your chosen instrument has a MIDI-controller version, as some wind instruments do. (Yamaha, as an example of one manufacturer, makes a MIDI wind controller, called the WX7, that produces no audio, but it's played like a sax and is easily learned by wind players.) Or you can use a simple keyboard for MIDI input. With MIDI's incredible flexibility, you don't need to have stellar keyboard skills. You can enter data slowly, correct flubbed notes, and even use a "correct on input" mode for poor timing (called *quantization*).

Keyboards for All

The recommendation of this book is to purchase a keyboard as a MIDI input device, no matter what your keyboard skills are or how many actual keyboard instruments you plan to use in your music. Of all the musical instruments in the world, the piano-style keyboard is the most ideally suited for a variety of musical input tasks, including MIDI. Besides, you can dust off your "Chopsticks" riffs during those creative lulls.

You don't need to purchase a behemoth full-blown synthesizer to get a workable keyboard with some decent MIDI-input features. You can get a compact MIDI keyboard that has no sound-generating circuitry of its own (which is a good thing when looking for an inexpensive MIDI controller) and use the sounds from your computer to listen to your performance. Keyboard controllers are made by many manufacturers, including Edirol and M-Audio, whose PCR-50 is shown in Figure 2-5.

Figure 2-5
M-Audio's Keystation49 provides versatile MIDI control features but offers no internal sounds, which keeps the cost very affordable— about $160.

You're encouraged to create music using your input device in the most musical manner possible. If you like to perform at the bottom of a canyon, on the altar of a cathedral, or in the smoke-filled basement of a cabaret for your sound, please do so. At the end of the day, though, remember that all music destined for recording ends up on a wire. What you do with the end of that wire is the next step in the signal chain: connecting to an interface.

Interfaces

Interfaces are where the magic happens between the world of music and the world of computers. A screaming death-metal guitar riff or the sweet strains of a string quartet goes into an interface and somehow comes out the other side in a language that computers understand, and so it can be manipulated with great power and flexibility with software tools by you, the user. Then this edited data goes back through the interface, back into the analog world of loudspeakers and human ears, where it's restored to its earth-shaking or sublime glory—with your edits incorporated. The interface is the great translator.

Interfaces come in many forms, including built-in interfaces, as in the case of the Macintosh, which sports stereo mini-jacks for input and output right on the computer's case, and the integrated audio chip on many Windows computers, including those from Dell. But there is a lot of versatility in interfaces, and computer musicians often opt for a third-party interface as a rule, not relying on the built-in audio in their computer. The choice for an interface varies depending on your specific audio needs, but we'll explore a couple scenarios that will help sort out which is right for you.

Interface Configurations

Perhaps the easiest way to begin understanding the wide world of interfaces is knowing their different physical forms, or *configurations*. Following are the three primary interface configurations, or physical ways an interface hooks up to your computer.

Soundcards

The simplest, cheapest, and oldest of the interface configurations is the *soundcard*. A soundcard is a collection of chips and other electronic components on a flat circuit board, or *card,* that plugs into the PCI slots inside your computer case. The card has jacks (connectors) that stick out the back of your computer's case and remain exposed after you insert the card and close the case back up. You then plug your instruments and other music-making devices into these jacks. Very often a computer comes with an included soundcard, which is just fine to get going on your recording projects, though you may find you want to upgrade after a while.

The process of installing a soundcard is simple. Just follow these steps:

1. Remove the soundcard from its packaging and note that it has ports that will protrude out of the back of your computer and gold tabs that will insert into the PCI socket on the motherboard, as shown in Figure 2-6.

Figure 2-6
Your soundcard has ports on one side and gold tabs on the bottom.

2. Open your computer, choose an open PCI socket that the card snaps into, and then work the card into position, making sure the ports will stick out of the back while simultaneously lining up the tabs with the socket, as shown in Figure 2-7. Figure 2-8 shows a close-up of the tabs going into the socket. Because the tabs are in two unequal sections, it's impossible to stick the card in backward.

Figure 2-7
The card is almost ready to be inserted into the socket.

Figure 2-8
The tabs are in position, ready for insertion.

3. Press down gently but firmly with both hands, as shown in Figure 2-9. Be careful not to rock the card in any direction, but rather press it straight down.

Figure 2-9
Press the card firmly into place, and you'll feel a slight snap, indicating a good fit.

4. Reattach the mounting-plate screw to secure the card, put the cover back on, and your computer will now look like Figure 2-10. The ports remain exposed so that you can make computer-data and audio connections.

Figure 2-10
The back of the computer, after installation and with the case closed back up, reveals only the card's jacks.

Soundcards with Breakout Boxes

A variation on the soundcard is the soundcard with breakout box. Because there are only so many connectors you can physically cram onto the exposed plate of a soundcard, interface makers quickly devised the breakout box to accommodate more jacks and other circuitry. The breakout box is connected to the computer's card with a special multiwire cable and can be conveniently placed (which the back of a computer can't always) in a case or rack that is 19" wide, the standard measurement for rack-mounted audio gear. A breakout box often has switches and knobs for added control over the sound, even before it hits the computer. Figure 2-11 shows the Delta 1010 system from M-Audio, a breakout box, and a PCI card.

Figure 2-11
The M-Audio Delta 1010, a breakout box with cable and soundcard

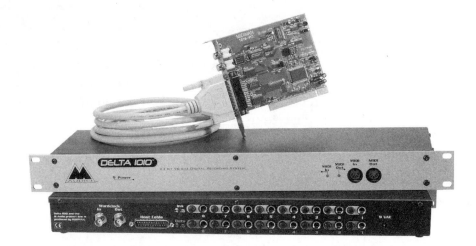

USB and FireWire

One of the most welcome improvements in computer communications ports is the jettisoning of the traditional multipin serial and parallel ports in favor of USB and FireWire. In addition to standardizing the hook-up procedure for peripherals such as keyboards, mice, printers, and scanners, USB works very well for audio and MIDI. You can't do heavy-duty audio multitrack work with USB because it's only reliable for about four tracks of simultaneous audio, but that's enough for a lot of projects, or even a session that might not need more than four tracks of simultaneous audio until a later time.

FireWire (also known by its engineering name, IEEE 1394) has been included on all Macintosh computers for some time but is easily fitted to Windows machines with a PCI or PCMCIA card (less than $40 and $30, respectively, at the time of this writing), and it's much faster than USB. Consequently, FireWire can handle pro-level multitrack projects, but it's used on more expensive interfaces.

What's nice about USB and FireWire is that no cards are involved, so they're much easier to hook up. You just plug them into your computer's appropriate ports and you're done; no messing around with opening the case. It also means that one interface can be shared between a desktop and a laptop with no additional hardware. As icing on the communications cake, both USB and FireWire devices are *hot-swappable,* meaning you don't need to power down your computer and restart it to hook up or swap peripherals.

When going with a USB device, you can purchase inexpensive two-channel audio interfaces or go with the higher-end four-channel devices that include more controls and features. Beyond four channels, USB isn't fast enough to support a simultaneous audio stream reliably. That's when you consider FireWire interfaces, such as Mark of the Unicorn's 828 and 896. Their operation is not much different from USB: You just plug them in, install the software from the CD-ROM, and start passing audio through your system. USB has enjoyed an upgrade to 2.0, so it will be a viable communications protocol for audio and MIDI for some time. FireWire is gaining in popularity due to MOTU's efforts and high-end devices from Digidesign and RME.

Figure 2-12 shows a popular USB-based audio interface, the Edirol UA-1A, which transfers up to two channels of audio simultaneously. You can plug anything into this interface—such as a keyboard, a mic preamp output, a drum machine, or a mixer output—and then plug the USB cable into any available USB port in your desktop or laptop computer.

Figure 2-12
The Edirol UA-1A is
a simple, two-channel
audio interface that
converts any analog
audio signal into
digital audio and
feeds it to the
computer via USB.

Audio Interfaces

Now that you know the physical configuration of interfaces, or how they actually hook up to your computer, let's look at the different types of interfaces available from a functional perspective (i.e., the different tasks they perform). An interface, regardless of whether it's a soundcard, breakout box with card, USB, or FireWire, can perform a variety of duties involving audio, MIDI, and other digitally controlled signals (such as synchronization). Also, many devices can perform *all* these tasks, which could make your interface a one-stop shopping solution for all your signal-routing and -processing needs.

Analog Audio Interfaces

Analog audio is what comes out of your mic or instrument cable. It's what you would plug into a P.A. system or an amp, if you were playing live. But now we're in the digital recording world, so this signal needs to be converted to digital data to be recorded onto a computer. Inside an analog audio interface are analog-to-digital converters, chips and circuitry that turn continuously fluctuating voltages into discrete digital chunks. When audio is converted into digital data, two specifications are considered: the sample rate and the bit depth. The sample rate is how many times the converter *samples* (takes digital snapshots of) the incoming signal. Just as film projection involves moving a series of still photos past the eye fast enough to simulate continuous motion, so too is digital audio playback a series of frozen sonic images that, played sequentially at a fast enough rate, appears continuous.

Several sample rates exist, but the CD spec is 44.1 kHz (kilohertz), or 44,100 samples per second. Once these samples are captured, the next spec that comes into play is how to store them. A single sample at 16-bit resolution (*16 bit* means 2 to the 16th power) has a range of 65,536 different places to represent that signal. Higher sample rates and bit depths exist, and musicians are pushing to get these better formats as part of our available listening choices, but for now the CD spec of 44.1 kHz/16 bit is what all music must eventually become (even if it was originally recorded at higher and better sample rates and bit depths) if it is to be listened to on a conventional CD.

An audio interface, at the very least, must be able to convert analog audio into a format of stereo channels (separate paths) at 44.1 kHz/16-bit digital audio. The interface also must have circuitry to perform the converse operation—taking digital data and converting it to the analog audio understood by speakers, headphones, and other analog equipment (such as cassette decks). This twin conversion circuitry is known as an *A-D/D-A converter.*

Digital Audio Interfaces

Not all the signals you'll deal with in your recording activities will necessarily be analog. Sometimes the analog-to-digital conversion will be handled for you, before you even get to the interface or computer. For example, if you use a digital mixer or multitrack digital tape machine (such as the Alesis ADAT or TASCAM DA series) to gather and wrangle your signals, you may be presenting your computer with an already-converted signal. DAT decks and some CD players feature digital outputs as well as analog ones, and it's more convenient and hassle free to simply transfer a digital signal to a computer than to try to record it in the analog fashion (where you must consider and set recording and playback levels).

For situations where your signal has already been digitized, you'll use a digital-audio interface. These don't feature the familiar 1/4" jacks and mini-jacks that are seen for analog connections. Instead, you'll see RCA jacks (like those used on stereo systems, but these handle digital signals), a fiber-optic connector called Toslink, and computer-style D-sub connectors (those multipin, trapezoid-shaped plugs).

Figure 2-13 shows a simple digital-audio interface, the ADAT Edit card. Its audio jacks are the tiny black holes on the right—one for input and one for output. Because these are optical connections, they can hold a lot of data on a tiny wire—eight simultaneous channels of digital audio, in and out. The computer-style plugs are for synchronization, which is necessary when performing transfers (playback and recording) between two digital machines.

Figure 2-13
The Alesis ADAT
Edit card is a simple
digital interface card
that uses Lightpipe,
or eight channels of
optical-format digital
audio on each
fiber-optic cable.

Analog/Digital/Clock

It's much more common in audio interfaces to find a combination of analog and digital connections, because most recordists' setups include both analog and digital sources. If you have digital connections, you must have a sync port, and that can be in the form of a Word Clock connection (a separate signal that ensures two machines will lock together) or sync ports, which talk to the machines' internal synching signals. An analog/digital interface will contain analog connections (in the form of 1/4" and RCA jacks), digital audio connections (RCA, computer-style D-Sub, or Lightpipe), and Word Clock (BNC connector) or sync ports. Figure 2-14 shows the back panel of the MOTU 828, an interface with both analog and digital audio connections for digital audio transfers between two digital machines.

Figure 2-14
The MOTU 828 has
analog and digital
connections to handle
a variety of audio
signal sources
found in typical
computer-studio
setups.

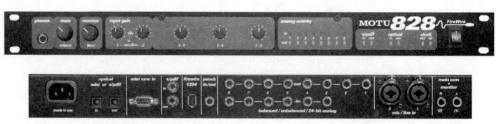

Audio + MIDI Interfaces

MIDI is vitally important to digital music production for producing musical notes as well as adjusting parameters and controlling other functions. Most interfaces past a certain point of sophistication include MIDI jacks along with their audio capabilities. This way, you don't have to employ a separate box for MIDI functions, and you don't use up another port on your computer just for MIDI. All digital information, audio and MIDI, share the single USB or FireWire cable of one device. MIDI connections from your instruments plug into the interface via circular, five-pin jacks, and the MIDI information is then commingled with the audio data onto the USB or FireWire cable.

Multipurpose Interfaces

The deluxe approach to interfaces involves seeking out a box that will do everything: analog and digital audio conversion, MIDI I/O, sync and Word Clock interconnection, mic preamp processing, and monitoring duties (provided by a headphone jack with its own level control). Having one unit that performs all these interface functions reduces the number of boxes and cables that will clutter your studio. This is a good idea for housekeeping, and it prevents the gremlins that plague audio components as their numbers increase—the hum, noise, and general degradation that occur as signals pass in and out of boxes with differing circuitry. An all-in-one, self-contained box eliminates conflicts and resists outside interference, making digital life cleaner as well as simpler.

Figure 2-15 shows the MOTU 896, which has a large number of jacks, plus the horsepower to process digital and analog audio for multitrack operation, MIDI I/O, preamps and phantom power circuitry for plugging condenser mics in directly, and sync and Word Clock ports for digital synchronization between devices.

Figure 2-15
The MOTU 896 is a pro-level interface with onboard mic preamps, synching capabilities, audio and digital I/O for multitrack recording/playback, and extensive I/O versatility.

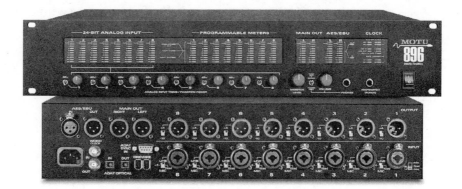

Control Surfaces

The concept of an interface isn't limited to converting signals from one format to the other. An interface also allows other kinds of translations, such as human impulses into computer-controller data. The alphanumeric keyboard was the earliest of computer interfaces, allowing people to type data into the computer. The mouse quickly followed, as a different sort of interface, preferable to a keyboard in many graphically oriented environments. In music production, we as recordists need an interface that will translate our musical moves as well as perform the relatively passive task of converting signals. For controlling and changing musical parameters, we now have the *control surface*, a digital controller that works with data but is not limited to audio conversion, and excels at the human approach to data control.

A control surface looks much like a conventional mixer: It has knobs, switches, and sliders (faders), because these are the best controls for human hands to work. The movements of these various controls are translated into the necessary digital language to, say, raise and lower the volume of a signal smoothly, boost the high frequencies of a channel, or turn on and off the mute status of a channel. Controllers work with audio and MIDI, parameter tweaking (EQ and pan), and transport control (Start, Stop, Rewind, etc.), enabling you to keep your hands away from the computer while performing more musical and mixer-like tasks. A controller is not a substitute for a full-blown mixer, because it translates data only into and out of the computer. A controller is not self-contained in the way a mixer is; it needs a computer to function.

Controllers are becoming extremely popular among desktop musicians, so there is a wide range of models to fit a variety of budgets. At the lower end is the TASCAM US-422 ($249 list), a USB device that features two tracks of simultaneous audio transfer as well as MIDI control of transport functions and parameters. At the high end is the Digidesign Digi 002 ($2,499 list), shown in Figure 2-16, which uses FireWire, can transfer multiple tracks of high-resolution audio, and has motorized, moving faders, and a whole host of deluxe features.

Figure 2-16
The Digidesign
Digi 002 works with
FireWire and is a
fully professional
system with
motorized faders
and other high-end
features.

Outboard Mixers

Though you have all the mixing capabilities you need inside your computer for desktop recording, an outboard mixer is sometimes a very convenient thing to have, either as an A-D converter or as a way to premix signals before going into the computer. If you decide to go with a digital mixer, it will be the most expensive component in your studio, more expensive than the computer itself. But it will help you add effects to your signals without spending precious CPU resources, and often digital mixer A-D converters are as good or better than the ones you may have on your soundcard or other interface. A smaller, analog mixer is handy for grouping like signals, such as four or five mics that you're using to record live drums. Used this way, a mixer is referred to as a *submixer* and is not used to replace the software-based mixer but rather to assist it by pregrouping some signals.

You don't need to buy a mixer for its ability to mix or to increase any inherent mixing versatility in your desktop studio; you have all that already, right in the mixer window of whatever software multitrack audio recorder you're using. But if you happen to have an outboard mixer lying around, you can integrate it successfully with your computer-recording setup simply by taking the stereo outputs of the mixer and treating them as you would the signal from a keyboard or drum machine. Figure 2-17 shows the signal path of an outboard (external) mixer integrated with a computer recording setup.

Figure 2-17
A small, inexpensive outboard mixer can be used to group together the mics of the drum set and other instruments so that the signal is treated as a unit once it hits the computer interface. This saves valuable input space on the interface and allows the overall level control to be handled by the outboard mixer's master fader.

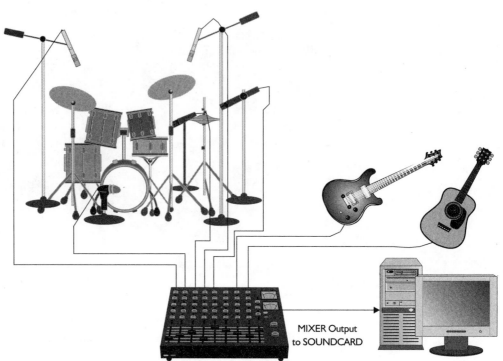

MIXER Output
to SOUNDCARD

Other Noncomputer but Essential Stuff

To get your computer recording system to work, you don't need anything other than the multimedia speakers that came with your computer or those you can purchase for less than $30 in any computer store. However, keep in mind you're creating music to be listened to from a CD and over a stereo system, not necessarily a desktop computer. When you begin to listen to your music critically, in order to make decisions in the balance of the elements and the tone controls, you'll want to be making those judgments using speakers that are much better than the kind that may match the color of your monitor but are less than stellar in their audio performance.

The process of listening back to recorded music is called *monitoring,* and the speakers you use are referred to as *reference monitors,* or just *monitors,* for short. Monitors for music production are different from those sold for stereo and hi-fi systems. They're much more robust as far as handling a wide range of signals, and they're more accurate in their reproduction of what they see at their input. Stereo speakers are often "tweaked" so that the low frequencies "punch" and the high frequencies "sizzle." But this doesn't necessarily serve the musician trying to make a master recording that will play back on a variety of systems. For mastering, you want to hear your music as neutrally as possible, and that requires a more careful and expensive approach to loudspeaker manufacturing.

Monitors are not sold in stereo stores; they're sold in music and audio stores. Though you can learn a whole lot about the recording and mixing process without high-quality monitors, in order to get predictable and good results in your mixdowns, you'll need to invest in some decent-quality monitors designed for music production. Alesis, Genelec, KRK, Mackie, Tannoy, and Yamaha are just a few companies that specialize in making monitors for music mixing.

Figure 2-18 shows the Tannoy Reveal Active, a popular choice for a *powered* monitor (meaning it doesn't need an external power amp to drive it because the amp is built in). The Reveal Active is built like a tank (and won't blow up or fail with repeated use and long hours of loud signals pumping through it), and a stereo pair of them provides the neutral, accurate sound desired by desktop recordists.

Figure 2-18
The Tannoy Reveal Active is a medium-priced monitor (about $750 per pair) that's good for *nearfield* (where the listener is only a few feet away) monitoring purposes.

Budget Speakers

I realize that $750 for speakers may be beyond the financial pale for many recordists, especially when there's so much other gear to buy. If you want to go the inexpensive route, consider a set of multimedia speakers that includes a subwoofer, which is a dedicated speaker for handling just the low frequencies. It's often the low end that gets sacrificed in budgets systems, so by making sure you have a separate subwoofer, you can control your bass frequencies somewhat.

The Altec Lansing Ultimate 621 series costs only about $150 and provides pretty good sound (see Figure 2-19). If those pro-level speakers must wait until another birthday, the 621's will do just fine.

Figure 2-19
The Altec Lansing 621 speakers feature a separate subwoofer and provide good sound for recordists on a budget.

Headphones

Much cheaper than a high-quality set of monitor speakers is a pair of headphones. Headphones are good for zeroing in on sounds, to listen for specific problems or strange happenings in your mixes, and are handy when you have to do some basic, or *rough,* mixing and can't crank up your speakers. Headphones are silent to those in the immediate vicinity, and this has two advantages for computer recordists: they keep sound in, meaning no one hears what you hear, and allow you to keep working when someone is sleeping nearby. Also, they keep external sound out, which is important when you need to concentrate on a particular passage to see whether the guitar part is in tune with the second baritone harmony vocal—something that's harder to judge over large speakers with all that air in between and perhaps two people chatting in the near vicinity.

Headphones are the tool of choice for editing on the micro level—trying to shave off the breath sound of the singer as she inhales just before her entrance. Headphone types include those with open or closed earpieces. The closed variety provides maximum isolation, completely surrounding the outer ear, but can become more uncomfortable over time. It's largely a matter of choice, but many recordists who use headphones for detail work opt for the closed-ear variety. Figure 2-20 shows the AKG K 240 DF headphones, a closed-ear system that works well for monitoring under critical situations. They cost only about $120 (street).

Figure 2-20
AKG K 240 DF
headphones feature
closed earpieces,
which completely
surround the outer
ear, resulting in
better isolation than
open-ear models.

Moving On

Having discussed all the outboard gear that helps your computer do its job, it's now time to delve into the heart of computer-based music production: software. Hardware is but a mere canvas compared to the artistry that software programs can splash on it. Chapter 3 discusses how applications and programs marshal all this hardware into music-making machinery.

Chapter 3

Building Your PC Audio System

Tools of the Trade

To complete this chapter you will need:

ATX-compatible minitower case with power supply

XP-compatible motherboard

AMD Athlon XP 2100+ (or better) processor with heat sink and fan

256 SDRAM memory module

Screws and standoffs for motherboard and drive installation

Maxtor hard drive with controller cables and installation disc

CD-RW and floppy drives and installation discs

Windows XP Pro operating system installation discs

Cordless screwdriver

Flathead screwdriver (handheld)

In Chapter 2 we explored all the wonderful possibilities for making music from a hardware perspective, but sooner or later you have to decide on one system and go with it.

In this chapter we'll follow the steps for building a PC optimized for home audio recording and music production. As we do, keep in mind that each choice presented is only one way to approach the process. There are many variations, depending on the specific components in your system.

However, the principles of building a system are reassuringly similar for all Windows-based machines, regardless of configuration. And some routines—such as installing processors, memory, and peripherals—are nearly identical on Macs and PCs. If you're savvy enough to be reading this book at all, you probably understand that. What I will try to do is point out, whenever possible, the musical significance in the available choices we have.

System Component Considerations

A system is an integrated collection of parts, and it's difficult to consider any of the parts in isolation. For example, though you start the building process with the case, you can't choose a case without knowing the type of motherboard you want, because cases come with predrilled holes according to motherboard types.

But you can't choose a motherboard without knowing the type of processor you'll have, because motherboards accommodate certain processors and not others (you can't stick a Pentium IV processor into a motherboard designed for an AMD Athlon).

So first decide on the processor type and speed you want for your music-production computer. This is how most people refer to the their computers anyway ("I have a 2.0 gig Pentium IV"). Then, budget permitting, choose either 256MB or 512MB of RAM and at least a 40GB hard drive.

When you have an idea of the basic requirements for your particular system, you can purchase the components all separately or in combination. For example, many cases will include a power supply, which saves the step of purchasing and installing one separately. Similarly, many processors come with the heat sink and/or fan already built in.

Case Studies

When choosing a case for your system, you'll need to consider several aspects. The first is what's called the *form factor,* which is just another fancy term for shape—or more specifically, shape, dimensions, and the compatibility with your motherboard.

The Minitower

Computer cases come in several different shapes—I mean *form factors*—but the best one for music is a minitower. It's not as monolithic as a server tower, but it's large enough that there's lots of open space for airflow, expandability, and accessibility. Also, it must be ATX–compatible (an industry-wide specification, observed by all computer manufacturers, that dictates the arrangement of the motherboard's components, such as the processor and the PCI slots), which most modern cases are.

I don't recommend a desktop case (the flat-looking box that you set your monitor on top of) because its horizontal orientation makes it less versatile with respect to drive bays and slots, and it's generally not as good for airflow. A server tower has lots of room, but it's pretty gargantuan unless you have just tons of room for it.

Legions of Fans

A minitower has more places to install fans than a desktop case, and this is something worth considering when you start to load up your case with peripherals and upgraded processors, which generate more heat. Also, because we're putting fans in our computer, and because fan noise is the enemy of critical listening, we're not going to place our case on the desktop—not for a monitor pedestal or anything else. Our computer is going on the floor or side of the desk, away from our ears.

HEADS UP!

Matching the Case, Motherboard, and Processor

Before purchasing any case, make sure it will accommodate your chosen motherboard. Obviously, this means you'll have had to make your motherboard decision first, and the motherboard you buy, in turn, has to accommodate the processor.

The case I bought for use in this project has four bays in the front, a slot for the floppy disk drive, and front-loading ports for two USB devices, a mic input, a headphone output, and a game port (see Figure 3-1). I'll be using only the USB and audio ports, but it's nice to have the others for possible future use.

Figure 3-1
The front panel of the project case has various front-access ports, which makes it more convenient to plug in temporary devices.

The case's back panel reveals six slots for various cards (AGP and PCI), plus additional ports for integrated components (i.e., built in to the motherboard), as shown Figure 3-2. In this case, I've removed the covers for the integrated components (the ones on the motherboard) plus the top slot in the PCI card location (which is where the modem will go).

Figure 3-2
The case's back panel reveals ports for integrated as well as add-on devices. The upper part of the case shows the power supply controls: the on/off switch, voltage selector (set here for U.S. operation at 115 volts), fan grate, and 3-pin AC power-cord port.

The inside of my project case has the power supply (upper left) already installed (see Figure 3-3) but nothing else, except for the empty cages (right) that will house the drives. You'll hook these multicolored cable bunches, which terminate into a white plug, to the motherboard and the disk drives. Other parts that need powering (such as LEDs) will take their current from the motherboard and don't connect directly to the power supply.

For this project, I opted for a 400-watt power supply, which is a safe bet for music production. You shouldn't use anything less than a 300-watt power supply for today's PC-audio requirements.

Figure 3-3
The inside of the project case, showing the power supply (upper left) and drive cages (right). The motherboard will go in just below the power supply, flush with the back (left side) of the case so that its integrated components' connectors will protrude out the back slightly.

Save a Step with an Installed Power Supply

Because many vendors offer cases with power supplies already installed, consider going with this option and saving yourself a step. Just make sure you get a power supply with at least 300 watts.

10 MINUTES

Step 1: Prepare the Case

Open the case by removing any screws that attach the left side panel (as you face the front of the computer). Lay the case flat on a workbench or table so that the motherboard mount is on the bottom (see Figure 3-4).

Check your motherboard to see what connections will stick out of the back of the case and then remove the metal covers by prying them off with a flat-head screwdriver. Be careful not to bend, twist, or distort the case in the process of removing the covers.

Figure 3-4
To prepare the case for installing the motherboard and other components, remove the left side panel and place the case flat on a table top. The power supply is in the upper-left corner; the drive cages (empty now) are along the right side.

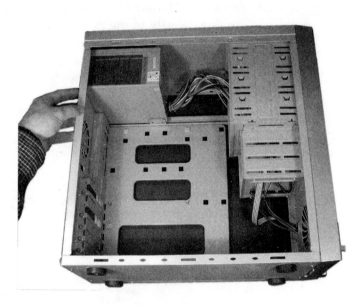

HEADS UP!

Discharging Potentially Harmful Static Electricity

Before touching, handling, or installing any of your computer's components, make sure you discharge any static electricity buildup from your body. You can purchase an inexpensive grounding strap that wraps around your wrist and attaches to the grounding screw of a wall socket plate, or you can periodically touch a metal doorknob, filing cabinet, or other metal object to release voltage that is potentially harmful to sensitive computer components. Keep memory and processor chips in their static-resistant bags until two seconds before you're ready to install them. And discharge yourself frequently before handling them!

Home Base: the Motherboard

The motherboard is the flat circuit board with the electrical stuff sticking out of it. It's home base for all your components. In addition to the stuff that comes already attached to the motherboard (such as the integrated components that stick out the back), it will hold the processor, the memory, the controller and power connections, plus any expansion cards, such as a PCI soundcard, an AGP graphics card, or an NCR modem.

When you're building a computer, the first requirement for the motherboard is that it accommodate the processor you've decided on. The motherboard will also determine the type of RAM (such as DDR SDRAM).

My project motherboard is an Amptron 810LMR, which takes the AMD Athlon processor, my choice for this project (see Figure 3-5). It's not a particularly deluxe motherboard, but it suits my budget-oriented purposes and has a solid reputation for quality and reliability.

This particular motherboard has only two PCI slots, which is not considered a lot, but for an audio-only computer, it's adequate. It also had the right configuration of integrated components for my budget, including integrated video for my monitor, so I didn't have to buy an AGP graphics card. Figure 3-5 shows the motherboard with its significant parts labeled.

Figure 3-5
The Amptron 810LMR motherboard is a good board for music and audio production for musicians on a budget.

NCR slot

AGP slot

PCI slots

Clip set

IDE controller ports

Power supply socket

Processor socket

Memory slots

20 MINUTES

Step 2: Install the Motherboard

The motherboard attaches to the case via screws and standoffs. Standoffs are brass sleeves that hold the motherboard to the case chassis like miniature pylons (see Figure 3-6). Screw the standoffs into the case at the precise location for your motherboard's particular holes, making sure to apply even pressure so that all the standoffs will be the same height. This ensures that the board will be perfectly parallel to the chassis.

Figure 3-6
Attaching standoffs
to the motherboard
mount is the first
step in installing
the motherboard.

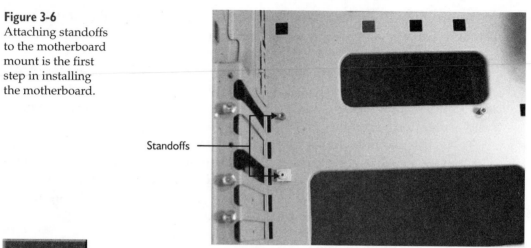

Standoffs ——

HEADS UP!

Removing Errant Standoffs to Avoid Electrical Shorts

Make sure you don't have any stray standoffs protruding from the case. If they come in contact with the motherboard's circuitry at any place except the designated spots, they could short out the board, causing permanent damage.

Before screwing the motherboard into the standoffs, place the motherboard on top of the standoffs and make sure that the holes line up and that the integrated components with ports sticking out of the back of the case all line up with the holes, as shown in Figure 3-7. At this point you can knock out any remaining covers on the case's back, if you haven't done so already.

Figure 3-7
Make sure the ports
will fit through the
holes in the back of
the case by placing
the motherboard
on the standoffs.

Begin screwing in the motherboard, applying equal pressure to all the screws so that the motherboard is perfectly parallel to the chassis. Check to see whether you'll be able to plug cables in and out of the rear ports without them catching on the case edges. As a final step, connect the power supply to the motherboard with the appropriate clip, as shown in Figure 3-8.

Figure 3-8
Completing the motherboard installation. After screwing the motherboard into the standoff centers, attach the power supply.

Integrated vs. Built-in Features

Part of the trick when choosing a motherboard is to assess the right integrated components. Integrated means the features are built in as part of the motherboard and will not have to be added later (for example, as an add-on through a PCI slot). You'd think that the more integration the better, but the fact is that integrated components are generally not as good as the PCI add-on variety. In a manufacturing irony, the fewer integrated components a motherboard has, the better it is for high-end applications.

For example, integrated video will not perform as well as a PCI video card or an AGP graphics card. So if you buy a motherboard with integrated video processing, then buy an AGP graphics card for better performance, you'll have paid for something you're not going to use. What's more, integrated components take processing power away from other parts of the computer, because they share the processor's power. PCI and AGP cards provide their own onboard processing and therefore don't tax the CPU for their tasks.

In practice, it's hard to buy a budget motherboard without integrated features, once you go below a certain price level. And I find it's handy to have integrated audio and video, even though I might supplant them with better add-on devices. It used to require a lot of expertise to disable the integrated processing in favor of a peripheral-based solution, but in Windows XP, it's easy and intuitive.

So don't fret unnecessarily about what integrated features your motherboard has. Focus on the processor, memory type, number of PCI slots (three as a minimum is safe, even though my project board has only two), and your own budget constraints.

My project motherboard has integrated audio and video, plus game, monitor, keyboard, mouse, USB, and other ports. One attractive feature was the integrated Ethernet port, which allows me to use my cable modem without having to give up a PCI slot. I'll need my PCI slots for FireWire and my soundcard.

The Brains of the Operation: the Processor

The single most meaningful component in a computer is its processor, or *CPU (central processing unit)*. This is the square-shaped chip that easily fits in and out of a special socket on the motherboard (see Figure 3-9).

Figure 3-9
The CPU chip and the socket on the motherboard that holds it.

For music and audio production, the choice of processors is down to two: Intel Pentium IV and the AMD Athlon. This excludes the budget versions from Intel and AMD—the Celeron and Duron, respectively—which aren't recommended for high-end audio applications. These chips will work, though, so if you already have a computer with a Celeron or Duron, don't worry too much. But if you're building from scratch or upgrading, consider only the Pentium and Athlon models.

Choosing between the Pentium and the Athlon is largely a matter of personal taste. The Pentium is more widely established, but the AMD is less expensive. Though there are technical differences between the two lines, these change with every update, and suffice it to say, I've never heard any musicians complain about either a Pentium or an Athlon not being up to the job.

The processor I selected for this project is the AMD Athlon 2100+ XP, which has a clock speed of 1.73 GHz. It's more than adequate for running a healthy arrangement consisting of multitrack audio, MIDI, and virtual effects. Faster processors are available (at this writing, up to 3.0 GHz), but I'm watching my budget, and because my music projects don't require more than about 16–24 tracks, the speed of 1.73 GHz is fine.

5 MINUTES

Step 3: Install the Processor

Though it's not brain surgery, you are dealing with your computer's brain, so you have to be careful when installing the processor and its heat sink. The following steps describe the installation process for the AMD Athlon, but it's very similar to working with Intel Pentiums. Be sure to consult the manual regarding your specific processor and heat sink before you attempt this important step.

1. Open the processor socket on the motherboard by releasing and lifting the silver locking arm. You'll have to move it slightly to the side first and then lift it up, so be sure to proceed carefully. With the locking arm in the up position, you're ready to insert the processor (see Figure 3-10).

Figure 3-10
Open the socket by pulling the locking arm to the side slightly and lifting it up.

2. Position the processor so that it's correctly oriented to the processor die (the square plastic frame with the holes). Note that the processor, even though it's a square, can be inserted into the socket only one way (check the pins in the corner and look at the corresponding holes on the socket). When correctly aligned and placed into the socket straight, the processor will slip right in with almost no effort.

3. Close the locking arm gently and tuck it back against the die, locking the processor in. The processor will shift slightly, but you shouldn't feel too much resistance. Figure 3-11 shows the processor seated correctly on the die.

Figure 3-11
The processor is locked and loaded.

Handling the Processor

The processor is a delicate piece of electronic equipment with zillions of fragile components packed into an object the size of a Triscuit. Handle it with extreme care, making sure you've discharged any static electricity from your body and avoiding contact with the pins on the underside of the chip.

⏱ 15 MINUTES   Step 4: Install the Heat Sink

All processors are covered by a heat sink, a radiator-like device whose function is to draw heat away from the processor. Not only can't you run your computer without a heat sink, but the heat sink has to be exactly, correctly installed.

Otherwise, you risk overheating the processor, possibly doing it permanent damage! Heat sinks have a fan that aids in the cooling process.

Installing the heat sink is not difficult, but it's a little trickier than installing the processor (which takes almost no effort at all). Following are the steps for correct installation of the processor heat sink.

1. Remove the paper cover over the adhesive-like pad on the bottom of the heat sink (the flat side). This exposes the *phase-change thermal compound*, which enhances heat transfer by making airtight contact with the top of the processor. The contact between the thermal interface material and the processor is absolutely critical, so don't let the exposed pad touch anything, and work quickly to place the heat sink over the processor.

2. With the indented portion over the right side of the socket, lower the heat sink steadily and evenly until it comes into contact with the processor. Hook one side of the mounting bracket over the plastic tabs. Use a screwdriver to help you push the metal bracket into place, if necessary. Then hook the other side of the metal bracket to the corresponding socket tabs. This will require exerting more force because the other side of the bracket is held in place by the tabs and offers resistance. When you've got both sides of the brackets locked in place, you're done! Your heat sink is held fast to the processor socket tabs and the phase-change compound is touching the top of the processor (see Figure 3-12).

Figure 3-12
The processor in the motherboard with the heat sink attached. While the processor slips right into the socket with little or no effort, attaching the heat sink's mounting bracket may require a little force to snap it into place.

3. Plug the fan's three-cord power cable into the appropriate power pins, located next to the memory slots on the motherboard.

HEADS UP!

Liberating the Heat Sink

It's easier to remove the heat sink than to install it. To release the bracket, you just have to "spring it" by using a flat-head screwdriver to pry the metal bracket off the tabs. Just be very careful not to slip and jab surrounding components on the motherboard.

Memories Are Made of RAM Chips

Memory is also referred to as *RAM (random access memory)* and is your computer's "working space." When you double-click an application, the computer loads it into RAM, where you create and edit your document. When you save to disk, the computer writes the contents of the RAM to disk, creating a more-or-less permanent record of your work at that point in time. Subsequent saves rewrite the file to reflect its current state in RAM.

Up until the time you save to disk, while the information is in RAM, it's not saved. If your computer crashes or you delete the material, it's gone forever. So it's a good idea to save to disk often. That way, in the event of a crash, you lose only the work from your last save (which shouldn't be more than a couple of minutes).

TIPS OF THE TRADE

Temporary Files

Some programs, such as Microsoft Word, save "temporary files" automatically, making the retrieval of files somewhat easier after a crash, but this is no substitute for saving frequently to disk.

In music, where performances are sometimes fleeting things, you should save after every performance, before going on and attempting any manipulation of that performance (though music programs save audio recording files as you record them) to keep the RAM from filling up during a long performance.

The more memory you can put into your computer, the more available tracks you have for recording and the more simultaneous effects you can have. Memory comes in the form of long, flat circuit boards, slightly larger than a piece of gum.

You specify your memory requirements in megabyte increments of 128, 256, or 512. Depending on the type of memory your motherboard takes (e.g., 168-pin SDRAM or 184-pin DDR SDRAM), a 256MB chip costs between $30 and $50. Not bad, considering the increased versatility it brings. After the processor, memory is the single most important component in boosting your computer's capabilities.

5 MINUTES

Step 5: Install the Memory

Figure 3-13 shows the insertion of a 256MB SDRAM memory chip into the appropriate slot. Notches on the chip help you line it up correctly in the slot, making it easy to see the proper orientation for insertion.

You can install as much memory as you have sockets for, and though I've installed only a single 256MB chip in my board, you're welcome to install another, giving you a very respectable 512MB of memory.

Figure 3-13
Place the memory chip into the socket with the gold tabs pointing downward. Press the chip into the slot gently and evenly so that all the gold-colored tabs go in together straight and not at an angle. When the chip feels seated, snap the side clips together to lock the chip into place.

TIPS OF THE TRADE

Playing the Memory Market

The price of memory fluctuates, so seek advice on when the best time to upgrade is. If you're in a hurry to upgrade but memory prices are running high, consider buying a lower-cost 128MB chip instead of the more expensive 512MB chip. Then wait for the prices to come down before buying a larger chip.

All About Disk Drives

Once you have the motherboard, processor, and memory installed, the next step is to hook up the drives. Following is a list of the three drives I've chosen for my PC recording studio:

❏   A Maxtor 60GB, 7200 rpm ATA/133. It has both the capacity (60GB) and speed (7200 rpm) for reliable audio performance.

❏   An Optorite 40×12×40 CD-RW drive.

❏   A generic internal floppy drive.

You can have a number of drives, but at the very least you need to hook up a hard drive; otherwise, you won't be able to run your operating system, launch any applications, or save data. The minimum requirement in a hard drive for audio is a spindle rate of 7200 rpm (revolutions per minute), which is a step up from the older 5400 rpm drives. The recommended seek time is 9 ms or under, which current drives have no trouble meeting. For this project, I've chosen a 60GB Maxtor drive that meets these specs, and for which I paid about $80 (see Figure 3-14).

Figure 3-14
This 60GB, 7200 rpm Maxtor hard drive provides ample capacity, seek time, and speed for audio applications.

Right behind the hard drive in priority is some sort of a removable media drive, preferably a CD-RW drive. Otherwise, how will you load in new programs or create audio CDs of your wonderful creations? I've chosen an Optorite 40/12/40 CD-RW drive. It will write to both CD-R and CD-RW formats. The three numbers separated by slashes refer to its different speeds for writing and reading. The first number refers to how fast the drive writes to the CD-R format (in this case, 40 times faster than real time). The second number is the rewrite mode, when you're using the disc for a subsequent writing in the CD-RW mode. The third number is the read rate.

20 MINUTES

Step 6: Install the Hard Drive

There are a variety of ways to install your drives, depending on the type of case you have. Sometimes you have to have remove the drive cage or bracket to install the drive; other times you can leave things where they are and just slide the drive mechanism in.

For this project's hard drive, I just slipped the unit into a lower shelf, leaving the power and controller connections exposed. I don't need front-panel access to the hard drive, so I put it in a location that has no removable front cover on the case. I secured the drive's position with four screws (see Figure 3-15).

Figure 3-15
Installing the hard drive on a lower shelf, where no front-panel access is necessary.

Connecting the Hard Drive

The hard drive connects through two cables: a power cable (actually a bunch of separate wires) and a controller cable, which is a flat, gray ribbon cable that transfers data and instructions. Following are the steps for hooking up the hard drive cables:

1. Hook one end of the controller cable (the gray ribbon-like one) to the hard drive, as shown in Figure 3-16. Note that the connector has a key that allows the plug to be inserted only one way into the port (which has a corresponding notch).

Figure 3-16
You hook the controller cable into the hard drive by aligning the cable's key with the hard drive port's notch.

2. Plug the other end of the cable (also keyed) into the ATA/133 controller port on the motherboard, as shown in Figure 3-17. Consult your motherboard manual for the correct primary IDE port that your hard dives connects to, if necessary.

Figure 3-17
The other end of the hard drive's controller cable hooks into the primary IDE controller port on the motherboard.

3. Take the power cable from the power supply and hook it up to its four-pin receptacle on the hard drive, as shown in Figure 3-18.

Figure 3-18
Complete the hard drive hookup by attaching the white plug from the power supply to the four power pins on the hard drive.

20 MINUTES

Step 7: Install the CD-RW and Floppy Drives

The CD-RW and floppy drives are installed from the front to allow for the inserting and removing of disks. The process is roughly the same for each drive:

1. Detach the drive bay covers from the case by pressing the plastic tabs that hold them into place. The CD-RW drive is wider than the floppy drive, so it will go in the wider, top-position slot. The floppy drive will go into the lower slot (see Figure 3-19).

Figure 3-19
Drives with removable media, such as CD-RWs and floppies, require front-panel access. Remove the drive bay covers and slide the drives in from the front.

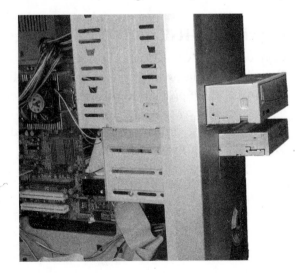

2. Slide the drives in gently until their faces are flush with the front of the case. Usually there's some leeway here, as the drives can go all the way back until they're stopped by the cage sides themselves, but that might be a little too far. So bring them forward a bit and then hold each one steady while you screw it in from the side (see Figure 3-20).

Figure 3-20
The drives are slid in and screwed in place from the side.

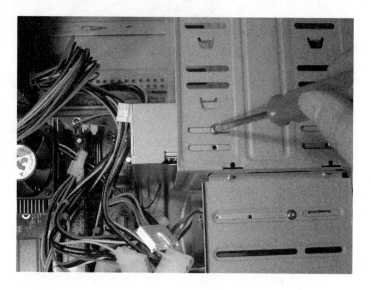

HEADS UP!

Aligning the Drives' Front Panels

If you're going to install more than one drive on adjacent shelves, make sure you can line up their front panels so that the top one doesn't ride up over the bottom one.

Connecting the CD-RW and Floppy Drives

Connecting the CD-RW and floppy drives is similar to connecting the hard drive. Each drive gets its own ribbon cable and controller port on the motherboard, and each requires a white-plugged cable from the power supply to provide it with power.

For the floppy drive, plug one end of the controller cable into the back of the drive and plug the other end into the motherboard using the port labeled "Floppy," as shown in Figure 3-21.

Figure 3-21
The floppy drive
controller cable is
connected from the
back of the drive
into its own port
on the motherboard.
In this case, it's
labeled "Floppy."

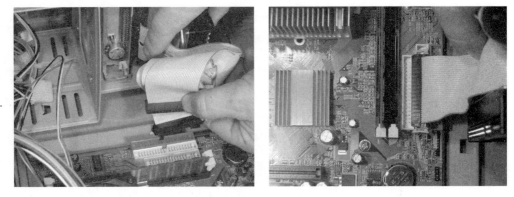

Hook up the power cable from the power supply into the back of the floppy drive, as shown in Figure 3-22. This connector is smaller than the one for the hard drive.

Figure 3-22
The power connector
inserted into the
floppy drive

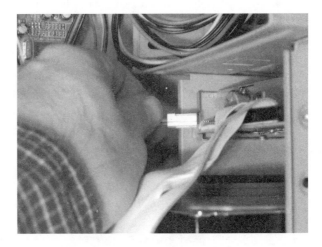

To connect the CD-RW drive, use a three-plug controller cable. Plug one end into the drive and the other end into the secondary IDE port on the motherboard, as shown in Figure 3-23. The unused connector can be used if you decide to add a CD-ROM drive later on. When you do, make sure to set its jumpers for slave configuration. Drives ship with their jumpers in the master position, and because that's what we want our CD-RW to be, we don't have to do anything to it.

Figure 3-23
Connect the CD-RW drive by hooking one end of the controller cable into the drive and the other into the secondary IDE port of the motherboard.

5 MINUTES

Step 8: Check Your Cable Connections

After inserting all your components correctly, take another check of the cable hookups. Whether it's a power cable (emanating from the power supply) or a controller cable (which connects to the motherboard), the receptacles are made such that you can hook them up only one way—the right way. So look at the shape of the plug and at the connector on the component, making sure it's matched to the pin configuration and that it's seated securely. Plugging in shouldn't require that much effort, and you'll know when you've established a good connection. If you're having trouble, check to see that the plug and port are at the right orientation to each other and that the pins themselves are straight. (They can get bent occasionally.)

Refer to the instruction manual that came with your motherboard to ensure that you're attaching the correct controller port to the desired drive. When you're all finished, the inside of your case should look like Figure 3-24.

Figure 3-24
The finished process, with all the cables hooked up. Some cables from the power supply remain unconnected, which is fine. They'll be used for future components.

With all the components in place, it's time to power up. All that's left to do now is to format the hard drive and install the operating system, which you'll do with the included CDs and the onscreen guidance of the installation wizards. To perform the next steps, you'll have to hook up a mouse and keyboard to navigate the various screens and options.

20 MINUTES

Step 9: Format the Hard Drive and Install the OS

For my hard drive, I used MaxBlast 3, the setup program from the manufacturer of my hard drive, Maxtor. It allowed me to format and partition the drive with an easy-to-use wizard. Remember, there's no operating system on the drive yet, so this operation can be achieved only with the hard drive's accompanying CD-ROM.

I then used the Windows XP Pro installation discs to install the operating system onto the hard drive, providing my name, password, and desired security and network settings.

I won't spend precious space on installing Windows, but if you have any problems at all, use Microsoft's online help system at www.microsoft.com/windowsxp and select the option that best addresses your issues or problems.

TIPS OF THE TRADE

Tracking the Changes to Your System's Registry File

Every time you install a device or make a significant change to your computer's setup, the Registry file is changed, stamped with the date and time the change was made. To troubleshoot effectively, if you ever have a problem, it's a good idea to restart your computer after each new setup change so that in the event you have to "roll back" to a state where things were working fine, you have a clear idea when that was. For example, instead of installing a new printer and infrared mouse in one session, install the printer first and make sure it functions properly. Note the computer's time for this successful installation. Then reboot and install the infrared mouse and its files as a separate step.

When your computer has a formatted hard disk and a working operating system on it, you'll just have to configure your system for the specific components you've installed, such as the CD-RW and floppy drives.

If you're using reasonably up-to-date devices from established manufacturers, Windows may already have the proper drivers resident on the hard drive from the installation process (this is especially true with printer drivers). If not, simply load the installation CD that came with your device into the CD-RW drive and follow the prompts in the Add New Hardware Wizard to find the appropriate drivers. After the wizard reports the successful installation of each device, be sure to test it by reading and writing data to it.

Moving On

Congratulations! You've built a working computer!

Now let's have fun with it and trick it out with some cool music-making tools. These tools are not like the screwdrivers you used in Chapter 3, and certainly don't require any manual dexterity to wield. I'm speaking of course of the software applications that we'll install to turn our computer system into a virtual multitrack tape recorder.

TESTING 1-2-3

At this point you should double-check to make certain the following items have been completed:

❑ The components and peripherals you've assembled for your basic computer system are hooked up correctly.

❑ Your hard drive is formatted.

❑ The Windows XP operating system is installed.

❑ All your peripherals are recognized and working properly, including the CD-RW and floppy drives, mouse, keyboard, integrated audio, USB devices (e.g., the printer), and monitor.

Part II

Building a Musical Arrangement step by step

Chapter 4

Recording on a Computer

N
ow that you've gotten your computer put together and Windows XP functioning, it's time to set up your audio and MIDI interfaces, install your software, and get your music system to make a joyful noise.

Though you *could* use the audio device that comes built in to your computer's motherboard, an interface that's specifically designed for music and audio production will offer superior sound and better performance in most applications.

The Audio/MIDI Interface

For this project, I've chosen the TASCAM US-428 as my audio and MIDI interface (see Figure 4-1). The US-428 provides excellent sound and can handle a wide range of audio sources, including microphones; instrument-level sources such as electric guitars and basses; and line-level sources such as home keyboards, synthesizers, and tape decks. It also offers four MIDI jacks (two in/two out, for 32 channels of MIDI), which will come in handy if I decide to expand my system with outboard synthesizers and other electronic instruments.

Finally, the US-428 is a great *control surface.* A control surface allows direct hardware control of many key audio features and allows me to set aside the mouse when working with my software mixer—a major timesaver.

Figure 4-I
The TASCAM US-428 control surface and audio/MIDI interface has real-time controllers for onscreen functions, AD/DA converters, and multichannel mixer capabilities.

The US-428 attaches to the computer via a single USB cable. You don't even have to open up the computer. Heck, you don't even have to reach around the back—just plug it into one of the front-panel USB jacks!

The US-428 has many other features, but we'll encounter them in context rather than trying to list them all here. In the projects we build in the next three chapters, we won't be tapping *all* of the US-428's capabilities, but it's nice to know they're there for future use. And though the US-428 is capable of rendering audio quality at 24-bit/48 kHz resolution (with audio specs, higher numbers are better), we'll limit ourselves to the CD standard of 16-bit/44.1 kHz resolution. This will save us a step when we go to burn CDs of our project.

10 MINUTES

Step 1: Install the Interface

Now that we find ourselves in the realm of software, the word "installing" doesn't mean what it did in the bad old hardware days (you know, way back in Chapter 3), where we pried open a metal case and poked around with a screwdriver. From here on, when we discuss "installing," it's usually in the software sense, where we "activate" a device by calling it up in a menu and selecting a radio button or checking a box.

I'll describe the installation of the US-428, but this procedure applies to any interface. When you install your interface, have the installation CD and the owner's manual handy.

To install the US-428, follow these steps:

1. Place the installer CD that came with the unit in your computer's CD-RW drive.

2. Take a USB cable and hook the square end up to the US-428's rear-panel USB port. Hook the narrower rectangular end to any USB port on your computer. Power up the US-428.

3. Follow the prompts in the Found New Hardware Wizard (see Figure 4-2).

Figure 4-2
When you hook up any new USB device, Windows XP will automatically sense it and present you with the Found New Hardware Wizard.

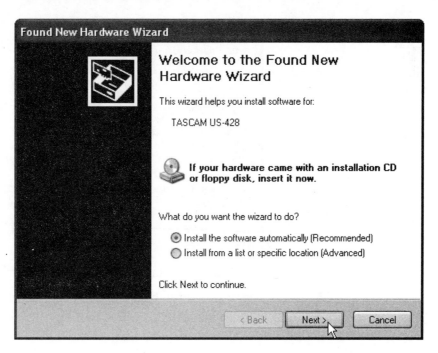

Found New Hardware Wizard

Welcome to the Found New Hardware Wizard

This wizard helps you install software for:

TASCAM US-428

If your hardware came with an installation CD or floppy disk, insert it now.

What do you want the wizard to do?

◉ Install the software automatically (Recommended)
○ Install from a list or specific location (Advanced)

Click Next to continue.

[< Back] [Next >] [Cancel]

After you follow the steps for installing the necessary software and drivers, your interface will be ready for operation. If the hardware wizard reports an error in the setup process, repeat the steps and read the prompts carefully. It's possible you may need to get an updated driver from the manufacturer's Web site.

TIPS OF THE TRADE

Downloading Updated Drivers via the Internet

If you're going to use a driver from the Internet (a common practice for receiving updates), make sure you've downloaded the file to a directory that you can navigate to easily later. This will save you the time of having your wizard scan the entire hard drive searching for the driver. Just use the Browse button to point the wizard directly to the new driver's location.

Testing the Interface

You can perform a check to see if the computer recognizes the US-428 by following these steps:

I. Select Start Menu | Control Panel | US-428 to launch the USB Control Panel, as shown in Figure 4-3.

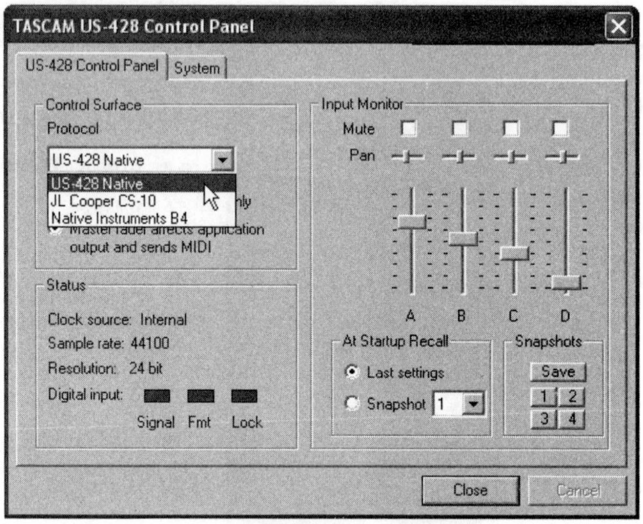

Figure 4-3
The TASCAM
US-428 Control
Panel, launched
from the Windows
Control Panel.

2. Select the radio button that reads Master fader affects application output and sends MIDI, as shown in Figure 4-4. This is under the pull-down menu with the field that should read "US-428 Native."

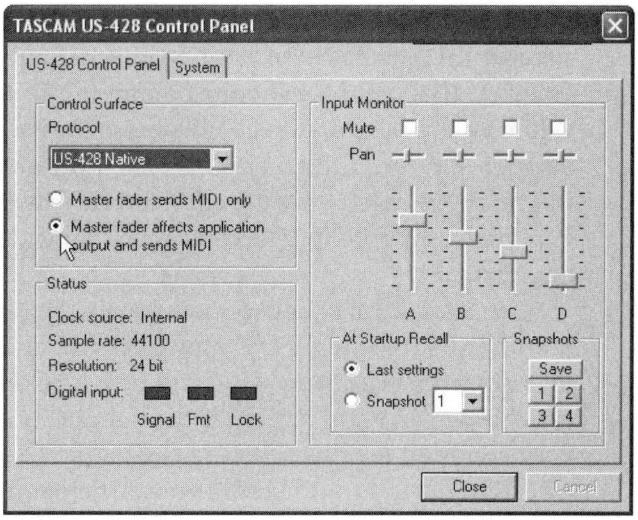

Figure 4-4
Select the second radio
button from the top,
just under the
pull-down menu.

3. On the US-428, press the switch labeled Input Monitor, which is located
on the right side, to the right of the rotary Pan knob, as shown in
Figure 4-5. The LED will light up green.

Figure 4-5
Press the Input
Monitor switch on
the US-428, which
lights up green to
indicate it's active.

On the US-428, move the first four faders up and down at random and look onscreen at the TASCAM US-428 Control Panel window. The onscreen faders, labeled A, B, C, and D, should be moving in tandem with your hand motions. While you're at it, on the US-428 press the Select button that appears just above Fader 1, lighting the green LED. Then press Mute above the Select switch and note that the onscreen Mute check box displays a check mark. Twirl the US-428's Pan knob and note that the onscreen Pan slider just above Fader A moves back and forth.

Congratulations! You've now finished installing the interface, and with that, your hardware interface is now in place, and you'll have some tactile control over screen parameters. This will be a nice alternative to reaching for a mouse every time you want to change the volume, pan, or EQ, or work the transport (all very common actions when recording).

All that's left to do before we start creating music is to set up the keyboard controller (for MIDI) and a microphone for vocals, acoustic guitar, or other acoustic sources.

The Master MIDI Controller

Your PC recording setup requires a MIDI controller for entering MIDI data, and the piano-style keyboard is the best available tool for this job—even if you can't play "Chopsticks."

The black-and-white keys are good for triggering the MIDI notes that drive synthesizers, samplers, and drum modules. The keyboard's knobs, sliders, and joystick are better for transmitting more continuous types of MIDI messages, such as smooth pitch bending, volume swells, and so on. The joystick even allows you to change two parameters simultaneously, such as raising the pitch while speeding up the vibrato—sort of the musical equivalent of rubbing your belly and patting your head.

The Project Keyboard

The controller I'm using for MIDI input is the Edirol PCR-50, a four-octave keyboard with a joystick and plenty of knobs and sliders for inputting continuous MIDI information. Besides being compact and having a great keyboard feel, the PCR-50 takes its electrical power from the USB cable—the same cable it uses to communicate with the computer. So it doesn't even need an external AC adapter; a single USB cable is all I need to hook the keyboard up to the computer. Figure 4-6 shows the Edirol PCR-50.

Figure 4-6
The Edirol PCR-50 is a four-octave MIDI keyboard with plenty of controls for MIDI data manipulation. It uses a single USB cable to communicate with the computer and draw power.

10 MINUTES

Step 2: Hook Up the Keyboard Controller

Because it's a USB device, the keyboard hooks up the same way as any USB device, such as a mouse or printer—just plug it in, wait for the Add New Hardware Wizard to pop up, and then click the Next buttons until the computer gives you the all-clear. Following are the steps to install and activate the Edirol PCR-50.

1. Load the PCR-50's installation CD into the CD-RW drive.

2. Connect a USB cable to the keyboard and the computer.

3. The computer will sense the presence of a new USB device and present you with the Found New Hardware Wizard, identifying the keyboard in the first window.

4. Follow the prompts for installing the device (including the directive to insert the installation CD in the drive, if you haven't done so already).

When you've completed these steps, you'll get a confirmation message that the device was successfully installed. Restart the computer. You'll now be able to access the all the music software installed on your machine with the PCR-50.

Making Audio Connections

Before the US-428 can send audio to and from your computer, you must connect it to the outside world. Inputs include microphone, instrument, line, and digital connections. Outputs include monitor outputs (for connecting to speakers), headphones, and a digital audio out (for interfacing with other digital gear).

Selecting a Microphone

Though it's not technically a computer peripheral, the microphone is one of the most important accessories in your PC-based studio. A quality, large-diaphragm condenser mic, such as the Audio-Technica AT-3035 (see Figure 4-7), does a good job of capturing vocals and acoustic instruments such as a guitar. Condenser mics are sensitive, so I try to isolate the mic from sources of noise (such as my hard drive) whenever possible.

Figure 4-7
A large-diaphragm condenser microphone such as the Audio-Technica AT-3035 can handle a wide range of audio material.

Unless it runs on batteries, a condenser mic requires *phantom power*, a 48-volt signal that reaches the mic via the three-conductor microphone cable. Although it has mic inputs, the US-428 doesn't offer phantom power, so I'll have to add a small phantom power supply between the mic and the XLR input on the US-428. I've chosen Stewart PM-1, which costs about $80 (see Figure 4-8). It may be an extra step, but it's worth taking for the quality that a condenser mic affords.

Figure 4-8
A phantom power supply is necessary when using a condenser microphone, but it's worth it for the quality.

Alternative Choices for Using an External Power Supply

You can avoid the added expense of a phantom power supply by using a dynamic mic, such as the popular Shure SM58 (about $90). Also, other USB interfaces include phantom power, such as various models by TASCAM, M-Audio, and Edirol. USB interfaces with built-in phantom power are becoming more and more common.

2 MINUTES

Step 3: Hook Up the Mic

To connect the mic, you'll need a special three-conductor mic cable, available at any electronics or music store. Unlike a standard audio cable, the mic cable has a different connector on each end. The end with the female XLR is the input; this is where you'll plug in your mic. The end with the male XLR is the output.

Plug the male end into your TASCAM US-428 or other interface. (If you use an external phantom power supply, plug the mic cable into the power supply first and use another XLR cable to connect the phantom power supply to your interface.) There are two XLR mic inputs, and because we don't have any other XLR connections, put the mic cable into Input A.

To check whether you have a signal, you don't need to hear anything, you just have to see that the Signal LED flickers, indicating a signal is present. Turn up Input A's Trim knob just until you see the green Signal LED under the Trim knob flickering in consort with your vocal checks.

HEADS UP!

A Condenser Mic Requires External Power
If you plug a condenser microphone directly into the US-428 without going through a phantom power supply, the mic won't work. It's not harmful to the mic or the interface, but it can cause frustration.

2 MINUTES

Step 4: Hook Up the Monitor System

Once you start stuffing your US-428 with all these great sound sources, you'll want to hear what they sound like coming out the other side. The US-428 has monitor outputs for both speakers and headphones, and they have independent volume control.

Hook up a set of powered monitors (ones that don't require a separate power amp) to the rear-panel jacks labeled Line Out. These jacks are RCA, so you'll need cords where one end is a male RCA and the other fits into your particular speakers.

Have a set of headphones on hand for critical listening and keeping the music away from sleeping housemates. You'll use this monitor system for both your inputs (instruments and microphones) and track returns (music coming out of the computer). And many times those will be happening simultaneously, so don't scrimp—get a good pair of headphones (such as the AKG K 240 DF model, about $120) and a set of heavy-duty reference monitors ($120–$1,500). (For more on monitors and headphones, see the section titled "Other Noncomputer but Essential Stuff" in Chapter 2.)

HEADS UP!

The US-428 Is not a Stand-Alone Mixer
Although the US-428 is a modern marvel, it does not function as a stand-alone mixer. It must be hooked up to the computer (and the computer must be turned on) to pass audio from its inputs to its outputs. There are other control surfaces on the market, such as the Event EZbus, that can function as stand-alone mixers, and do work without the aid of a computer.

5 MINUTES

Step 5: Install the Music Software

Once your mic and keyboard are plugged in and working, it's time to install your music software. I've chosen Steinberg Cubase SX because it offers a clean interface and enough features to cover almost any music-production job, short of CD burning. (It doesn't hurt that Cubase SX is among the most popular music applications in the world.) Many of the concepts we discuss in the following section can be applied to other products, such as Cakewalk Sonar, Cubase SL (an affordable alternative to SX), Digidesign Pro Tools, Emagic Logic Audio, and Mark of the Unicorn Digital Performer.

The first step is to install Cubase SX onto your computer. If you've purchased the program on CD, load the disc into your CD-RW drive and follow the manufacturer's instructions.

Cubase SX uses a hardware key as copy protection; without the key, the program will not run. Because the key fits into a USB port on your computer, be sure you have one available. You may need to add a USB hub to increase the number of USB ports.

You can also download a demo of Cubase SX by logging on to www .steinberg.net. As with the drivers, be sure to save the installer to a location on your hard drive that will be easy to find.

10 MINUTES

Step 6: Reboot and Launch the Music Software

With the software installed, it's time to reboot the computer. This allows Windows to load the Cubase SX files that operate on the system level. Then launch Cubase SX and finish setting up the studio. When you first launch Cubase SX, it will ask to test your audio system. You can skip this step because we're going to set up the audio system manually.

When it opens, Cubase SX shows you an empty screen, save for the menu bar at the top. Later, we can set the program to take us to an existing file, but first we need to configure Cubase SX to work with our audio and MIDI devices.

15 MINUTES

Step 7: Configure the Audio Driver

Like all audio software, Cubase SX communicates with the interface via a special piece of software called a *driver*. When I installed the US-428, it added a number of drivers to my computer, including MME and WDM drivers for working with Windows. Cubase SX can work with standard Windows drivers, but it performs better under Steinberg's own ASIO (Audio Streaming Input and Output, pronounced *AZ-ee-oh*) driver.

TIPS OF THE TRADE

The Importance of Low-Latency Monitoring

Low-latency drivers are important in multitrack recording because they allow you to hear your live playing delay-free and in perfect sync with your previously recorded tracks.

To configure the audio driver, perform the following steps:

1. Open the Devices menu and select Device Setup at the bottom of the window, as shown in Figure 4-9.

Figure 4-9
Cubase SX's
Devices menu lets
you configure its
various components.

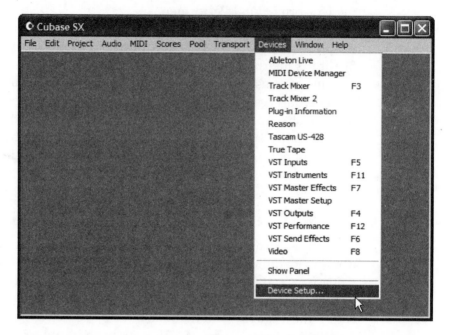

2. Once in the Device Setup window, go to the left column and select VST Multitrack, as show in Figure 4-10.

Figure 4-10
The VST Multitrack
tab in Cubase SX's
Device Setup window
allows you to select
and configure your
audio driver.

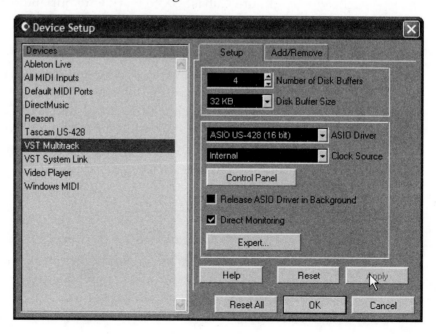

3. At the ASIO Driver pull-down menu, select US-428 (16 bit). Under the Clock Source menu, choose Internal. This allows Cubase SX to act as the master digital clock. You can access the US-428's internal settings directly by clicking the Control Panel button, which opens the TASCAM US-428 Control Panel, shown in Figure 4-11.

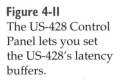

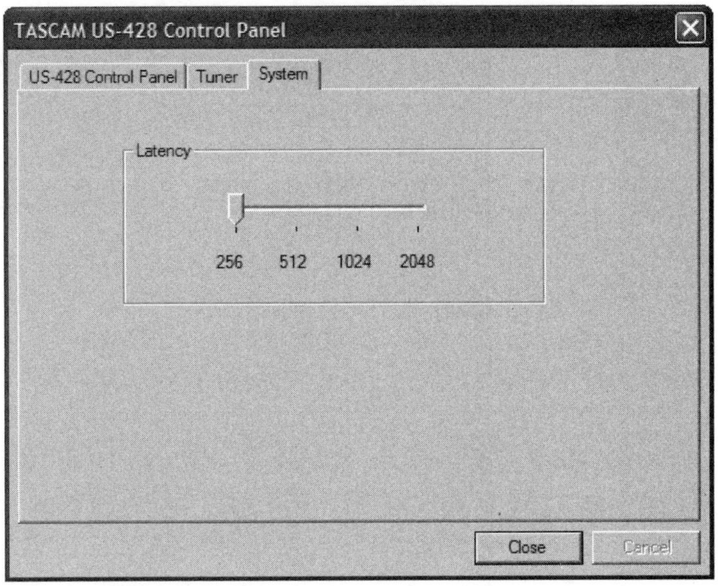

Figure 4-11
The US-428 Control Panel lets you set the US-428's latency buffers.

4. Click the System tab and set the latency to its lowest value, 256. Low latency can increase the strain on your computer's CPU, causing dropouts, but you can always return to this control panel and increase the latency buffer. Close the Control Panel and return to the VST Multitrack screen. Check the box next to Direct Monitoring. This allows you to hear the source signal (the one plugged into the US-428) without any latency.

TIPS OF THE TRADE

Monitoring Through the Mixer

Direct Monitoring bypasses Cubase SX's internal mixer. If you want to monitor your input signal through the mixer (desirable if you want to hear effects as you record), turn off Direct Monitoring and set the audio buffer to the lowest possible setting.

5. Click Apply and then click OK. These settings will be active for all songs you open in Cubase SX, but they can be changed at any time.

5 MINUTES

Step 8: Set Up the MIDI System

After setting the audio system, stay in the Device Setup window and navigate to the Default MIDI Ports' Setup tab (see Figure 4-12). Select All MIDI Inputs. This will allow both the Edirol PCR-50 and the TASCAM US-428 to input MIDI to Cubase SX.

Set US-428 Port 1 as the MIDI output. Cubase SX is capable of using a number of MIDI inputs and outputs simultaneously.

Figure 4-12
Cubase's Default
MIDI Ports window

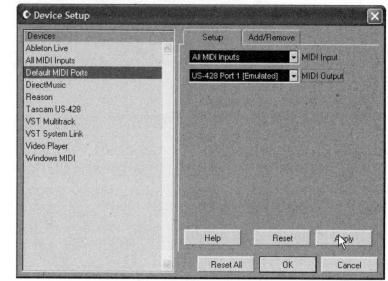

Finally, we'll set Cubase SX to communicate with the US-428 as a control surface. Click the Add/Remove tab in the Device Setup window and select TASCAM US-428 from the list, as shown in Figure 4-13.

Figure 4-13
Adding the
TASCAM US-428 as a
control surface

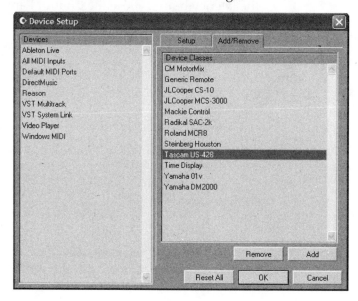

Now, click the Setup menu and set the MIDI ports for the US-428. You'll notice a set of function keys. (These can be assigned to control specific features within Cubase SX through the Device Setup menu).

Once all your audio and MIDI devices are set up, click OK. Now we're ready to make some music.

Step 9: Start a New Project

2 MINUTES

Before we can start recording, we need to set up a *project file* to contain all our audio and MIDI elements. Go to the File menu and choose New Project. By default, Cubase SX asks whether you want to start with a blank document or open a template, which is a file that contains preconfigured tracks (see Figure 4-14). Templates are useful timesavers, but for now, we'll stick with a blank file. Cubase SX asks you to specify a folder on your hard disk that will contain both the project file and any audio files that go with it.

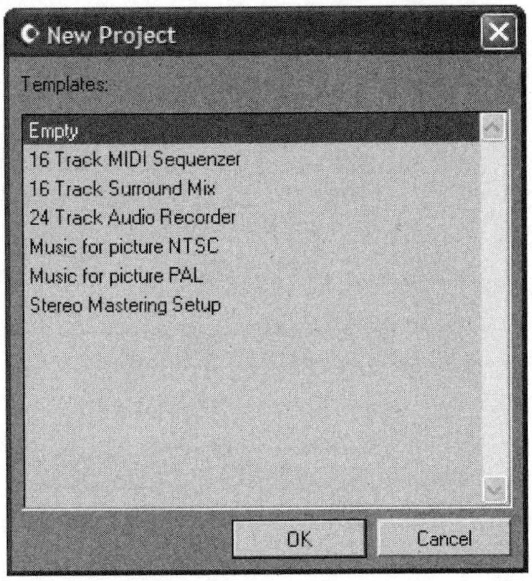

Figure 4-4
Cubase SX's startup screen gives you a choice between opening a blank document or a preconfigured template.

Each Cubase SX project can have its own settings for resolution and sample rate. To set these parameters for the current project, follow these steps:

1. Open the Project window and select Project Setup.

2. Set the sample rate to 44.1 kHz. This value will apply to all audio in the project. Cubase SX can only work with audio files that have matching sample rates. If there's a mismatch, Cubase SX will have to convert the files so that they match.

3. Set the resolution to 16 Bit (this should always match the settings in the VST Multitrack Device Setup window).

Whether you open up a template or start with a blank slate, Cubase SX opens the Project window and Transport Panel, shown in Figure 4-15. The Project window is the nerve center of Cubase SX, giving you access to all your tracks—and all the tools you need to work with them. The Transport Panel controls recording, playback, and location within the project.

Figure 4-5
Cubase SX's Project window and Transport Panel

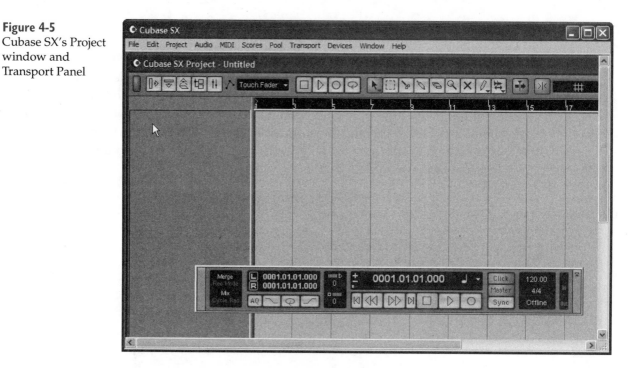

In the Project window, you can create new audio and MIDI tracks, set them up for recording and playback, and access the mixer to adjust the sound. This is also where you'll do most of your editing, which we'll tackle in Chapter 5.

TIPS OF THE TRADE

Recording at 24-Bit for Better Sound

Because the audio CD format uses 16-bit audio, we'll set our project's sample rate for the same value, so that we can create projects that don't require conversion when it's time to burn our work to CD. However, in many cases you can achieve better results if you record and process your audio files at a 24-bit resolution and then convert down (called *dithering*) to 16-bit as a final step before burning to CD. (This process is described in Chapter 5, in Step 13: Bounce Your Final Mix to Disk.)

Project Window Geography

Like most audio software, Cubase SX organizes each project in a grid. The top line (see Figure 4-16) is called the Ruler. You can configure the Ruler to display several time formats, including real time (minutes and seconds) and bars and beats. We'll stick with the default setting of bars and beats because it makes it easier to work with MIDI data.

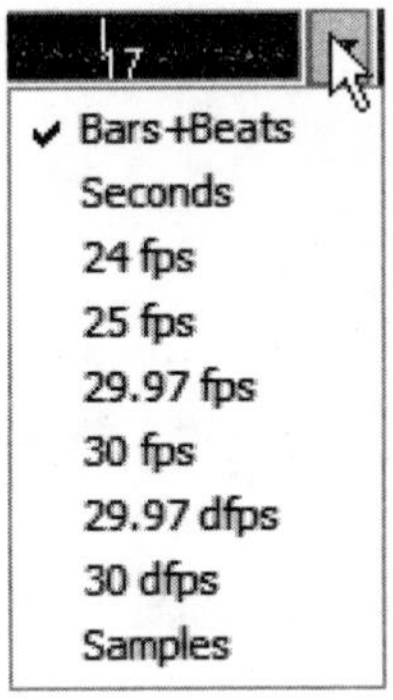

Figure 4-6
The Project window
Ruler, set to show
the song in bars
and beats

|17|
| ✔ Bars+Beats |
| Seconds |
| 24 fps |
| 25 fps |
| 29.97 fps |
| 30 fps |
| 29.97 dfps |
| 30 dfps |
| Samples |

Just above the ruler are Cubase SX's most important controls and switches: the Inspector, Tool Palette, Snap Settings, and Color Selector (see Figure 4-17). These are used to access track parameters, edit parts, and more.

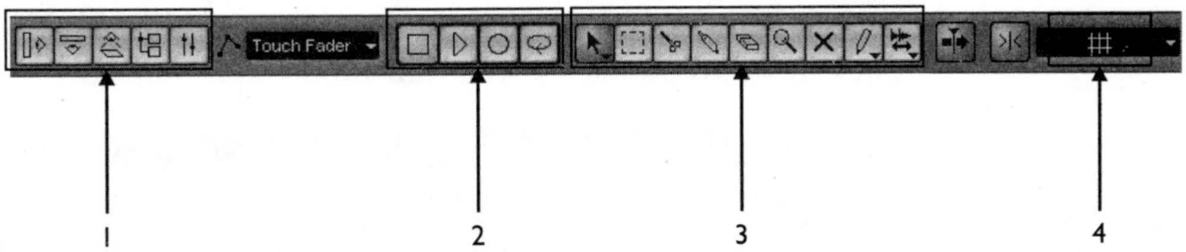

Figure 4-7
The elements above
the Ruler include
the Inspector (1),
Transport (2),
Tool Palette (3),
and Snap Settings (4).

1   2   3   4

10 MINUTES   ## Step 10: Create a New Track

Before you can record audio or MIDI, you must first create a track. Go to the Project menu and choose Add Track | Audio and—presto!—a new track called Audio 01 appears (see Figure 4-18). Notice that there's a red dot below the track name. This is the record-ready switch, which enables the track for recording. Cubase SX tracks can be either one channel (mono) or two channel (stereo). This setting must match the source material (in this case, mono).

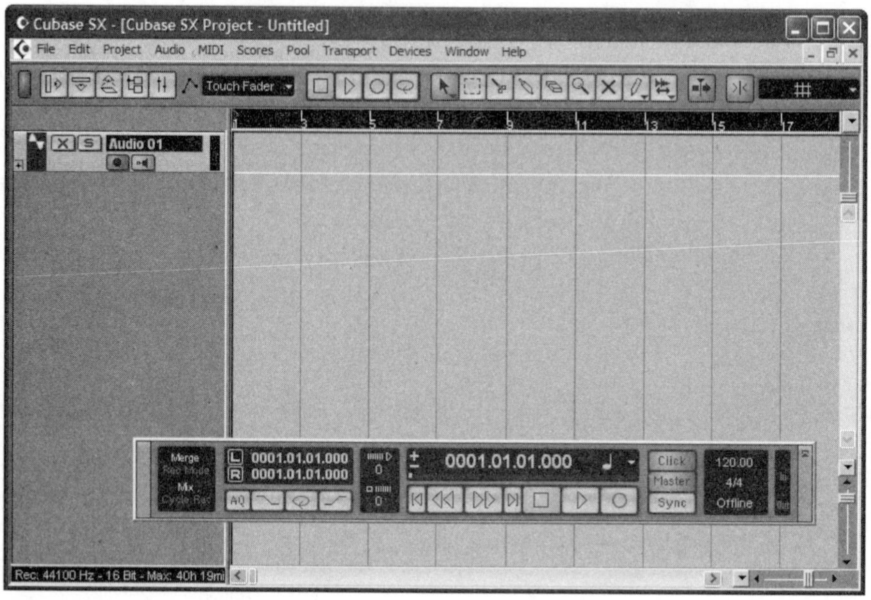

Figure 4-18
Adding a new audio track. Note that the red "record ready" button is lit, indicating that the track is armed and ready to record.

Before we record, let's name the track "Acoustic Guitar." Cubase SX will append the track name onto that of the audio file, something that becomes important when we start editing and exporting our audio.

So far, I've added a track, but I haven't given my song a title. I'm going to save my file as "BYOGW."

As we discussed earlier, the US-428 has four analog inputs, and we must assign the appropriate one to each track. Let's go back to the Devices menu, and select VST Inputs. This opens the VST Inputs window, shown in Figure 4-19. Click the Active switch for all four inputs.

Figure 4-19
The VST Inputs window lets you activate inputs for bringing audio into Cubase SX.

Click the Project window's Inspector icon. A column will appear to the left of the channel, showing a detailed set of controls for the track (see Figure 4-20).

Figure 4-20
The Inspector for the
Acoustic Guitar track

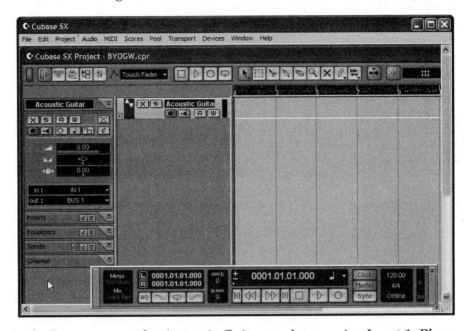

In the Inspector, set the Acoustic Guitar track to receive Input 1. Plug your microphone into the US-428's Channel A, turn on your phantom power supply, and start singing, playing your acoustic guitar, or making some other kind of noise. You should hear yourself through the US-428's audio outputs (speakers or headphones).

Notice the meter just to the right of the track name (see Figure 4-21). This shows the track's input level. Use the Trim pot on your US-428 so that the meter goes near the top when you play at your loudest but stays just short of the red zone.

Figure 4-2I
Input monitoring
using the software
meters in Cubase SX

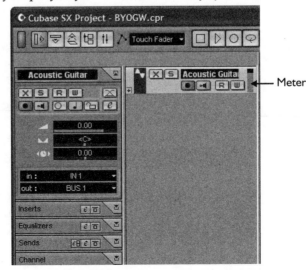

HEADS UP!

Checking that Cubase SX Is Receiving a Signal

If you hear yourself through the US-428 but the meter in Cubase SX doesn't fire, check that the track is set to the same input as your source and that the USB connection between the computer and interface is secure. If there's still a problem, go to Device Setup | VST Multitrack and click Reset.

TIPS OF THE TRADE

Beware the Dreaded Digital Clipping Syndrome

When you overload a digital input, you'll get a nasty distorted signal called *clipping*. This won't damage your computer, but it does sound terrible. A little overdrive in the analog world lends a certain warmth, but in the digital world, distortion is cold—and ugly. So be sure to watch that the signal never goes into the red, not even for a moment, or you'll risk ruining an otherwise perfectly good take.

The Transport Panel: Not Your Parents' Play, Stop, and Rewind

Appearing discreetly at the bottom of your screen, tucked into the corner of the flashier looking Project windows is the Transport Panel, the ignition that fires the Cubase SX engine.

The Transport controls are like tape recorder buttons on steroids. In addition to the usual functions you'd expect on a recording device, Cubase SX's Transport features Return to Zero for immediately snapping back to the project's zero point (which you can define). Its counterpart, Go to End, is helpful, too. Locators allow you to define points in a region, which you can jump to at the press of a button. You can loop the playback between locators.

In MIDI mode, the Transport Panel's various playback and record modes let you work in different ways. Cycle playback is good for rehearsing. When working with MIDI, Merge recording combines your playing with existing parts. In Cycle record mode, Mix overdubs each subsequent pass on the previous tracks (good for building rhythm parts), and Overwrite erases previous tracks, which is good for *woodshedding* (playing the part over and over until you get it right). If it helps, turn on Auto Quantize, which will clean up your rhythms upon input—no waiting until the editing stage to improve your timing.

Perhaps the best part about the Transport Panel is that you don't have to use it at all if you don't want to. Its functions are duplicated on your alphanumeric keyboard as well as your control surface. If you like working with a control surface, investigate all the ways to assign the function keys to access the Transport Panel's many modes and functions, and go online to see other tricks and shortcuts users have come up with.

5 MINUTES

Step 11: Record Your First Track

Now that we have a signal running into Cubase SX, we're ready to start recording. The next step is optional—but highly recommended for most forms of music. Go to the Transport Panel (see Figure 4-22), turn on Cubase SX's Internal click track, and set a tempo for your project.

Figure 4-22
The Transport Panel, with Click active and a song tempo of 120 beats per minute (bpm)

A click helps you play at a consistent tempo, which is especially important for working with MIDI and prerecorded audio files (such as drum loops).

Play along with the click and get comfortable with the track's tempo. If necessary, change the tempo by typing a new value in the Tempo Display.

Now I'm ready to click the Transport Panel's red button and record my first track, as shown in Figure 4-23.

Figure 4-23
The Transport Panel is in record mode, and Cubase SX is tracking audio.

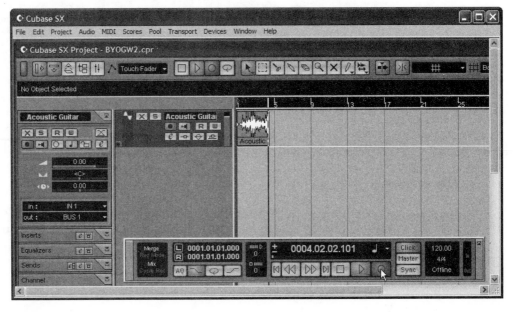

Using Keystroke Equivalents for Common Commands

You can access most Cubase SX commands via your computer keyboard. The default key for record is the asterisk; the default for play/stop is the spacebar. The US-428's transport can also drive Cubase SX. The controls resemble those of a standard tape recorder.

When I hit stop, Cubase SX takes a moment to draw an image of the audio file, called a *waveform*, and then places it in the Project window, as shown in Figure 4-24.

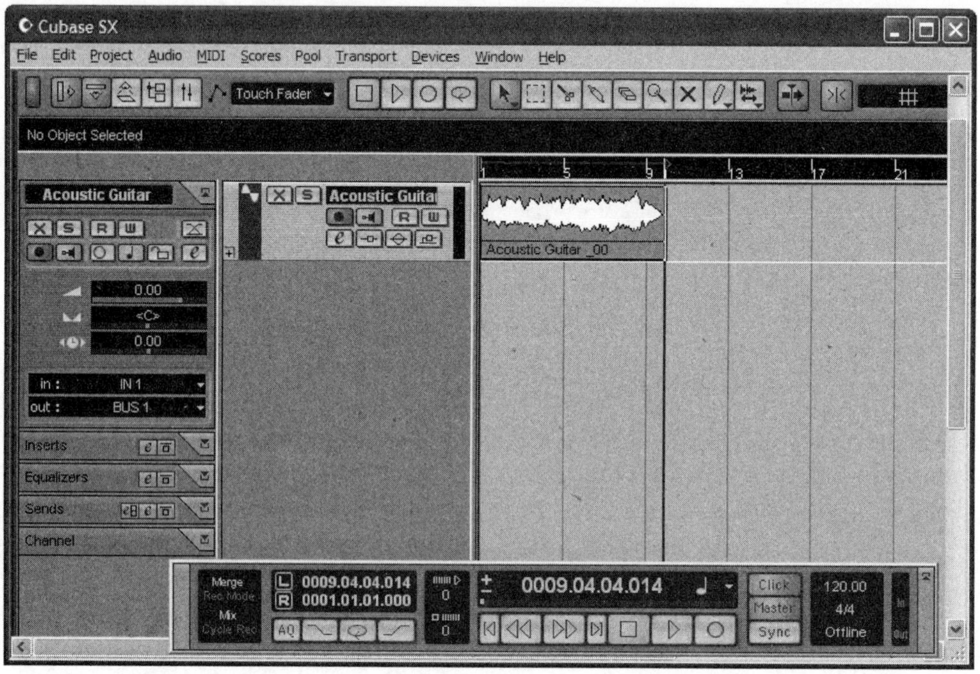

Figure 4-24
Our first track. Notice that the waveform display bears the name of the track, along with a number indicating the order in which it was recorded.

When Cubase SX records an audio file, it creates a special pointer associated with that file called an audio *event*. You can edit events without altering the original audio file—a technique called *nondestructive editing*. Each new event bears the name of the track, along with a number indicating the order in which it was recorded.

Your Second Take

Your first recording might have been mistake free, but mine wasn't, so I'm going to try a second take. With the track still record-enabled, I put Cubase SX into record mode and tried again. A new event appears superimposed on the first (see Figure 4-25).

Figure 4-25
Track 1, with a
second take in place

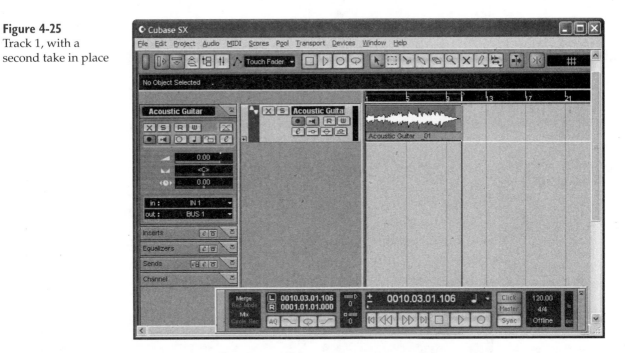

One of the coolest aspects of PC-based recording is that when you record a new take, the old one isn't erased but rather set aside for later use. Notice that this one is called Acoustic Guitar 01. This naming scheme helps me distinguish between the takes.

TIPS OF THE TRADE

Managing Your Accumulating Audio Files

Keeping files is generally good data insurance, but after you become proficient with Cubase SX, you may find you want to keep your project organized and save disk space by getting rid of these unused takes as you go along. Alternatively, you can leave them in place and delete them all in one fell swoop when you're finished with the project.

Hit the spacebar to initiate playback. This time, I nailed it, and I'm ready to move on to my next track.

5 MINUTES

Step 12: Record Additional Tracks

Now that I've recorded one good audio track, I'm ready to record more audio— a process called *overdubbing*. Let's go back to the Project window and select Add Track | Multiple. This will let us create a number of audio tracks at the same time. Select Audio from the Track pull-down menu and then type **3** in the Count pane.

TIPS OF THE TRADE

A Shortcut for Adding a Track to Your Project

You can also access the Add Track menu by right-clicking inside the audio tracks column of the Project window.

For Track 2, we'll add some bass to go along with the acoustic guitar. I've plugged an electric bass directly into Input C on the US-428 and set the US-428's hardware level switch to Instrument.

When I select Track 2 in the Project window, the track automatically arms itself, and its parameters appear in the Inspector. I'll name the track "Bass" and set it to receive Input 3 (see Figure 4-26). I then play the bass and check the levels, just as I did with Track 1.

Figure 4-26
I've added three more tracks and assigned one of the new tracks to Bass, receiving a signal from Input 3.

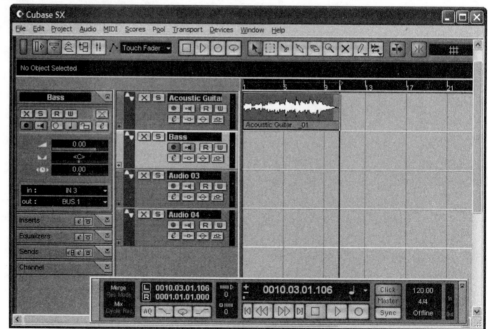

When I put Cubase SX into play and then plunk on the bass, I can hear both the bass and the acoustic guitar I've already recorded. Everything sounds good, so I go ahead and hit the Record button. The Bass event appears in the Project window (see Figure 4-27).

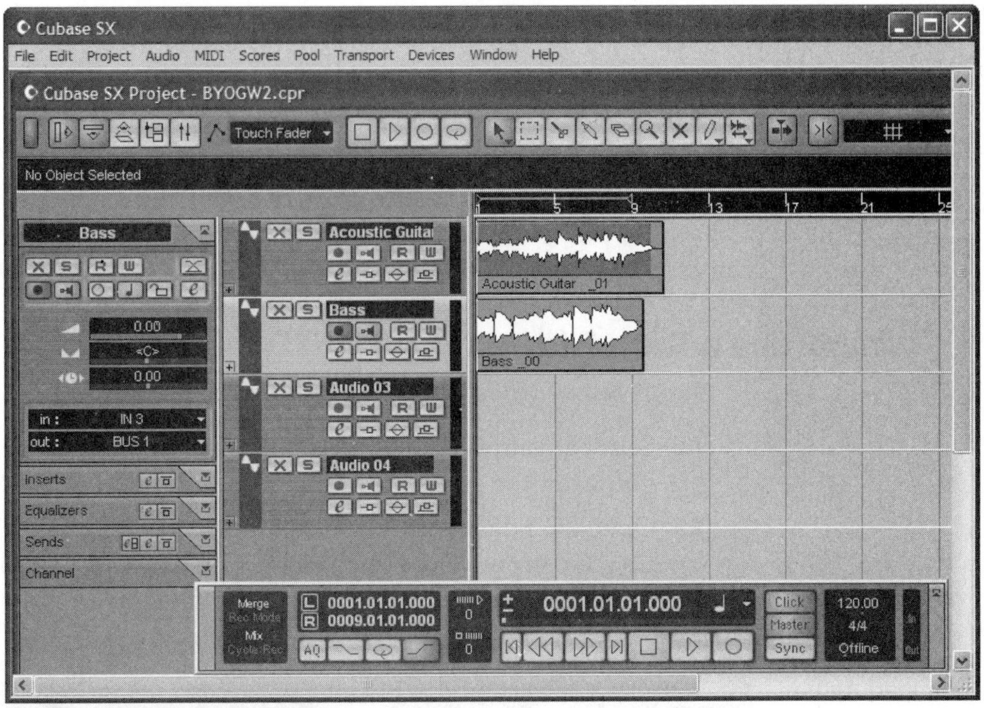

Figure 4-27
The bass track has joined the acoustic guitar track, indicating our overdub was successful.

I follow suit with an electric guitar and a vocal. Figure 4-28 shows the multitrack arrangement as it takes shape.

Figure 4-28
With four tracks in place, the "BYOGW" song is beginning to come together.

Step 13: Import Prerecorded Audio

Cubase SX can also work with prerecorded audio material, such as drum loops, sound effects, and parts taken from other projects. The audio you import into your project can come in two basic forms. *Data files* (AIFF, WAV, MP3, and other file formats) are the easiest to import because they're already in a form that Cubase SX can use. You can also take audio from an audio CD track. For this, Cubase SX must convert the audio to a data format, a process known as *ripping*.

Importing a Data File

To import a data file, perform the following steps:

1. Select an empty audio track and position the playback cursor where you want the audio inserted.

2. Open the File menu and select Import | Audio File. Cubase SX opens up a file browser window, where you can select and audition audio files, as shown in Figure 4-29.

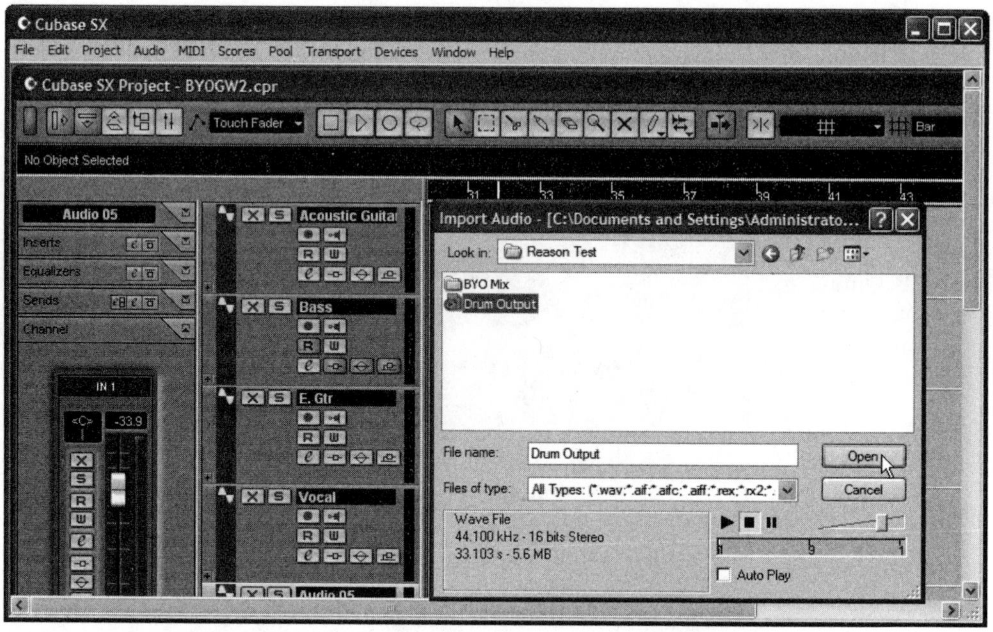

Figure 4-29
The Import Audio file browser. Notice the playback controls at the bottom right of the window. When you select a file, you'll see important attributes such as file type, sample rate, resolution, mono/stereo format, length, and site size.

3. Select an audio file. I've chosen a stereo drum loop.

4. Click Open. The Import Options window appears and asks whether you want to keep the file in its original location or copy it into the project folder. I like to keep all the elements of my projects in one place, so I'll check Copy File To Working Directory (see Figure 4-30).

Figure 4-30
The Import Options
window

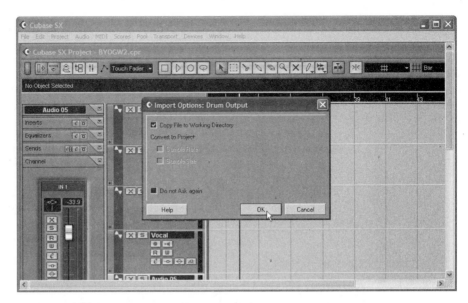

5. Click OK. Cubase SX will import the file to the selected audio track and set the track to match the mono/stereo status of the file.

Importing Audio from a CD

To import audio from a CD track, follow these steps:

1. Open the File | Import | Audio CD menu. The Import From Audio CD window appears (see Figure 4-31), listing the tracks on the audio CD, along with their length and file size.

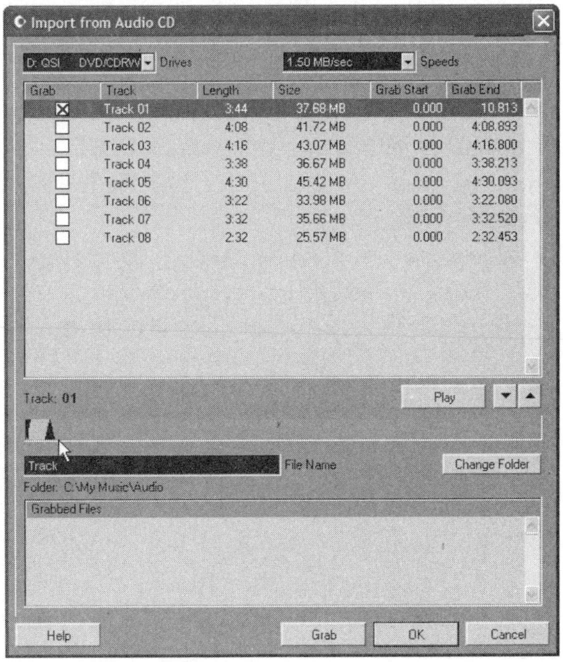

Figure 4-31
The Import From
Audio CD window

2. Check the box next to the track you wish to import. You can audition the track by clicking the Play button. The track will play back through the US-428.

3. You can use the slider underneath the Play button to set the Grab Start and Grab End parameters (upper-left corner of the window) to define how much of the track to take. I'm importing about ten seconds of audio.

4. Use the Track Name dialog box and Change Folder command to select a folder for the audio you're about to create.

5. Click the Grab button. Cubase SX will convert the CD audio to a WAV file, place it on your hard disk, and create an audio event in the Project window.

A Word about Tempo

Although you can bring prerecorded audio into any project, it helps when its tempo matches that of the material you've already recorded. Some sound libraries specify the tempo of each file so that you know in advance which will work in your project. If there's mismatch, the music will play back out of sync. Fortunately, Cubase SX lets you change the tempo of an existing audio file with a technique known as *time stretching*, which we'll cover in Chapter 5.

Introducing MIDI Instruments

You could create a very elaborate arrangement in Cubase SX without ever tapping into its MIDI features, but you'd be missing half the fun. MIDI is the ideal tool for working with electronic instruments such as synthesizers, drum machines, and samplers.

Cubase SX is equipped with a number of software-based instruments, known as *virtual instruments* (or VSTi's, for Virtual Studio Technology instruments), that emulate the hardware instruments you'd find in a typical keyboardist's rig.

You can also use MIDI to trigger external devices, such as real flesh-and-blood (or is it wire-and-silicon?) synths, but in the interest of staying within the PC realm, let's stick with the VSTi's.

5 MINUTES

Step 14: Launch a VSTi

Before we can record MIDI, we need to set up a MIDI track, route the keyboard controller to a MIDI sound source, and select a sound. Here are the steps to follow:

1. Go to Project | Add Track | MIDI. A MIDI track appears in the Project window underneath the last selected track, and the Inspector opens up showing the MIDI input and output assignments (see Figure 4-32).

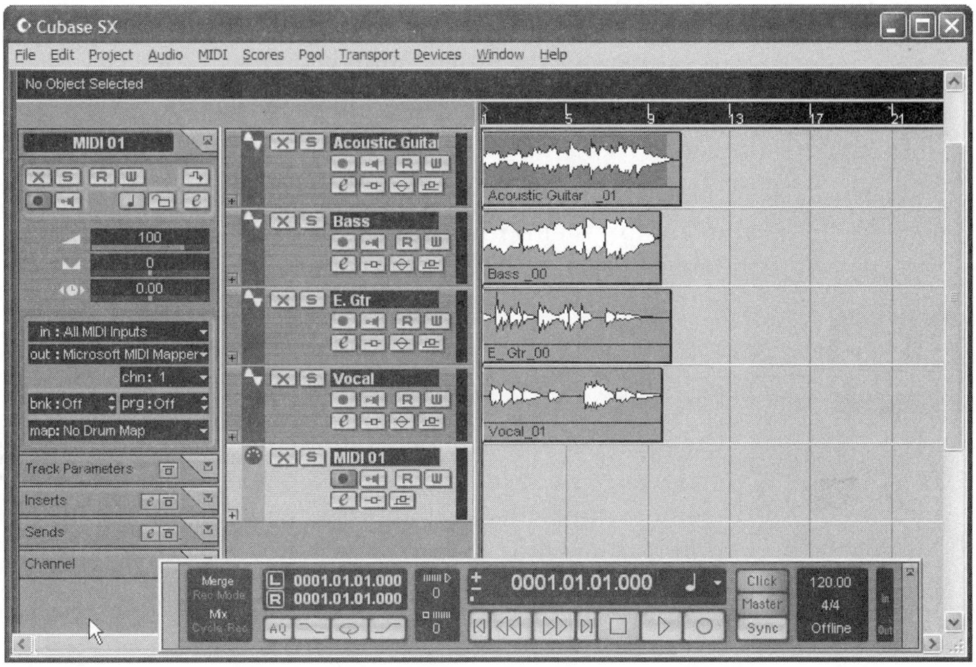

Figure 4-32
A new MIDI track in the Project window. Note how the Inspector here differs from that of the audio track in Figure 4-18.

2. Open the Devices menu and select VST Instruments. We're going to activate a synthesizer called the A1 Analog Synth Unit.

3. In the VST Instruments window, go to the A1's row and click the "e" (edit) button. The A1's control panel appears (see Figure 4-33).

Figure 4-33
The A1 synthesizer emulates a hardware analog synth. When you play your controller, the A1's keyboard (bottom of screen) plays along.

4. Open the pull-down menu at the top of the A1 screen and select a preset. I've chosen Warm Pad WMF.

5. Return to the Project window. Name the MIDI track and then set the output to A1 in the Inspector.

Now, when you play your controller, you'll hear the A1 playing back through your audio system. You can adjust the sound using the A1's controls or choose a different preset.

More than One Way to Work

Cubase SX offers a number of shortcuts and redundancies, giving you several ways to access important parameters. For example, the A1's preset menu is duplicated in the Inspector. Access it by clicking on the "prg." pull-down menu.

2 MINUTES

Step 15: Record a MIDI Track

Recording MIDI is similar to recording audio. You arm a track, press the transport's Record button (or the keystroke equivalent), and play along on your MIDI keyboard controller (or other MIDI controller). The result is a MIDI part, as shown in Figure 4-34.

Figure 4-34
A MIDI track with a newly recorded part

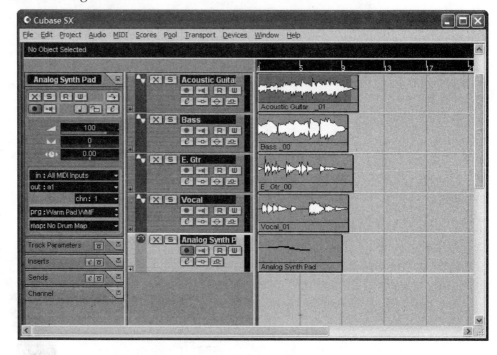

There are some important differences between audio and MIDI recording, however. By default, when you overdub MIDI, Cubase SX *layers* the new material on top of the previous material and combines them into one event. This can be very useful when you're building a part over several passes, but if you want to record alternate takes of the same part, you should open a new MIDI track for each take, assign each of these tracks to the same sound destination, and *mute* (turn off) the previous MIDI tracks (see Figure 4-35).

Figure 4-35
All these MIDI tracks are assigned to the same sound, but only the one on the bottom can be heard. I've muted the others by clicking the × icon.

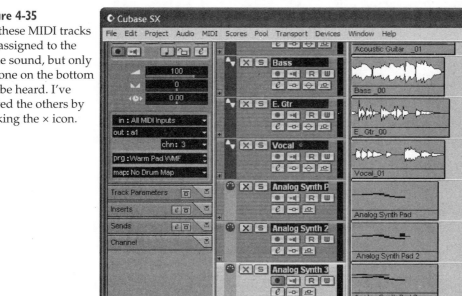

HEADS UP!

Choosing the Correct MIDI-Recording Mode

Cubase SX offers several different MIDI recording modes. Be sure you select the right one for your preferred mode of working. For example, if you want to experiment with adding successive layers to your previous passes, as you would in creating a multi-instrument percussion part, choose the Merge and Mix modes.

2 MINUTES

Step 16: Punch In a Segment

It often happens: You play the perfect take, but there's just one lousy note that fouls the whole thing up. To fix the problem, you don't have to rerecord the entire track. You can *punch in* and *punch out*, a technique that records only a small section of the track. Cubase SX lets you specify punch-in and -out points with the left and right locators. Figure 4-36 shows the Transport Panel and Project window ready for punch recording. The Electric Guitar track is record-ready. Recording will begin at the left locator and end at the right.

Figure 4-36
Preparing to
punch-in record

This is sometimes referred to as *auto-punch*. If you're recording others or using the punch-in process to rerecord a synched loop with a dropout, for example, you can simply press Record the old-fashioned tape-recorder way to punch in and then press it again to punch out without setting precise in and out points in the software. You can also use a foot controller with some software.

TIPS OF THE TRADE

Manual- and Auto-Punch Recording

Setting up locators so that you can perform hands-free punching is as also known as *auto-punch* in other software. You can punch in and out manually by activating Record while the music plays and then deactivating it when the section passes. Don't worry if you miss the punch—you won't erase any previously recorded material. You can also use a foot pedal with most software, allowing you to keep your hands on your instrument.

When I punch in a part, Cubase SX creates a new event within the locator boundaries. Note that the rest of my audio track is unaffected (see Figure 4-37).

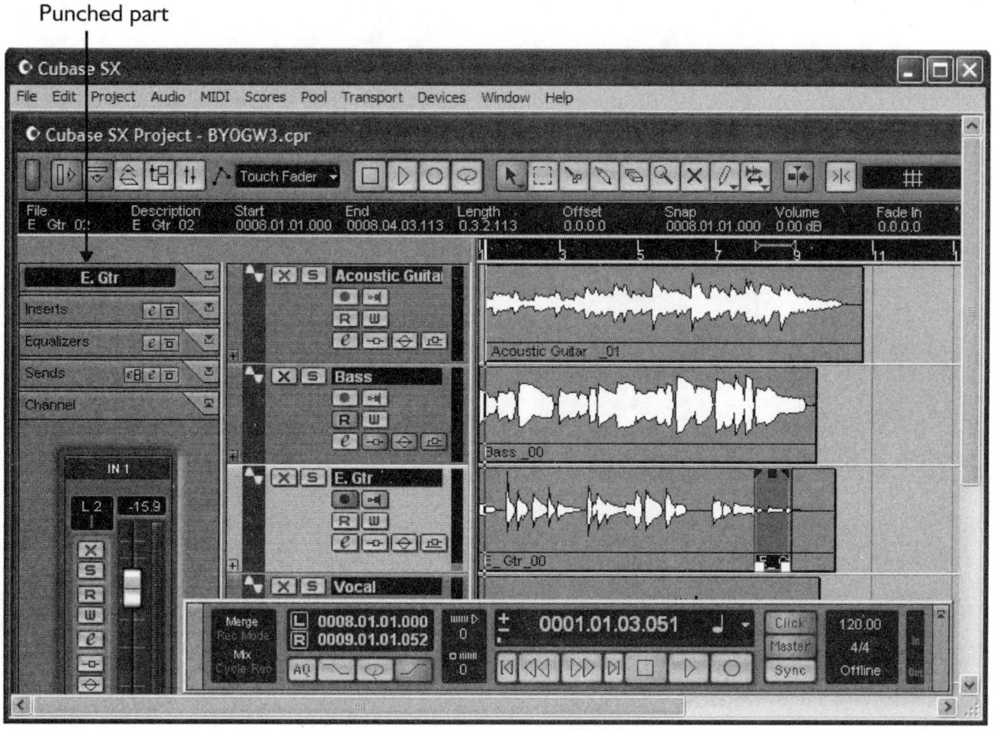

Figure 4-37
The Electric Guitar track after a punch-in recording. The shaded area shows the new material.

Punched part

Step 17: Record Multiple Tracks

5 MINUTES

So far, we've discussed recording one track at a time, but you can record as many simultaneous tracks as your hardware allows—essential if you want to record a band or to track vocals along with your guitar.

The US-428 lets you record up to four audio tracks simultaneously (you can also record MIDI at the same time). Plug each source into the appropriate inputs and assign each track a separate input. These sources can be additional microphones, a drum machine with its left and right outputs plugged into two channels, or electronic keyboards and synthesizers.

Arm multiple tracks for recording by holding down the SHIFT key when you click the Record Ready button. Figure 4-38 shows four audio tracks and a MIDI track ready to record.

Figure 4-38
Cubase SX is ready for multitrack recording.

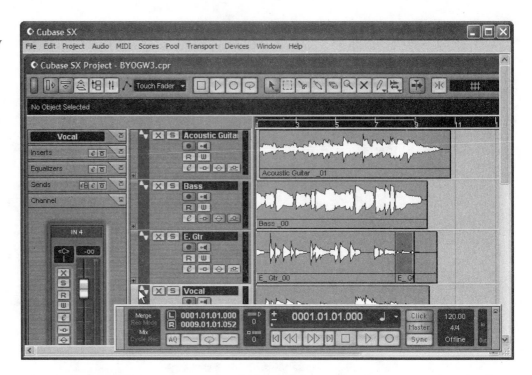

Then feed all your sources in by cueing the band to play or by playing the individual instruments yourself, one after the other, and watch as the project window fills in data in the appropriate tracks.

Moving On

Your computer is a powerful recording studio, but what sets it apart from conventional recording equipment is its ability to edit your recordings and automate your mixers. We'll explore more of these topics in Chapter 5.

At this point you should have completed the following items:

❑ Set up your interface to send and receive audio and MIDI

❑ Set up input sources, such as keyboard, microphone, and electric guitar

❑ Installed and configured Cubase SX

❑ Recorded audio and MIDI, each on an individual track

❑ Recorded additional tracks as overdubs

❑ Imported audio

Chapter 5

Editing, Mixing, and Processing Your Music

Tools of the Trade

To complete this chapter you will need:
A multitrack project with audio and MIDI tracks
Your hands
Your ears

In Chapter 4 we set up a studio and started tracking audio and MIDI. Hopefully by now you've put together the beginnings of a good song and, in the process, developed a feel for Cubase SX.

But getting the tracks onto disk is only the beginning of the production process. The middle—mixing and editing—is where you'll tap into the true power of the PC-based studio.

Before we begin, a brief aside. PC-based production includes a wide range of activities: audio recording, MIDI recording, editing, mixing, arranging, and many other techniques that combine these processes. Though I've separated these steps (in order to introduce them more clearly), they need not follow a specific sequence. I often start mixing and editing the minute I've recorded my first take—setting levels, adding effects, setting EQ, and trimming excess parts. By the time I'm ready to "mix," the job is nearly done. Good housekeeping along the way saves you the procrastinating engineer's copout, "We'll fix it in the mix."

Mixing Your Tracks

Anytime you work with a multitrack arrangement, even one as simple as my project song, you must mix the project down to make it playable on a stereo audio CD.

To create a stereo mix in the hardware world, I would need to connect a multitrack machine to an outboard mixer and then connect the mixer to a stereo mixdown deck. But with Cubase SX, these elements are built in.

Cubase SX's Track Mixer (see Figure 5-1) sports most of the controls you'd find on a traditional hardware mixing console, but it's designed to work within the computer environment and can handle both audio and MIDI tracks. You'll find individual channel strips (these correspond to your recorded tracks), an effects section, and the busses (common paths that signals can be grouped to) that output your mix to its final destination.

In addition to the Fader, Pan, Mute, and Solo controls, each audio channel includes an Equalizer (EQ, for short) control for adjusting the tone, a Sends control for accessing bus effects, and an Inserts control for adding individual channel effects. MIDI channels are equipped with a similar set of controls, though these are designed to manipulate MIDI data in real time.

Figure 5-1
Cubase SX's Track Mixer includes channels for each audio and MIDI track, as well as a master output fader.

You don't have to open the Track Mixer window to access a channel's mix controls. Clicking the Channel tab in the Inspector (see Figure 5-2) opens the mix channel for the currently selected track, complete with Fader, Pan, Mute, and Solo controls.

Figure 5-2
The Inspector showing the mixer channel for the Bass track

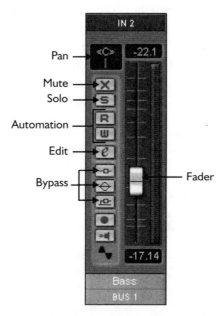

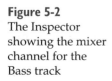

Step 1: Set Levels

The best way to get a feel for the mixer is to make some moves and hear how they sound. Start playback and click the Fader with the mouse (or use your US-428 or other control surface). Slide it up to make the track louder, down to make the track quieter.

TIPS OF THE TRADE

Loop a Section to Hear Repeated Playbacks

When mixing, it's often useful to hear the same section of music repeat over and over. To loop your playback, put the Transport Panel into Cycle mode and set the locators to define a section of the mix.

Next, adjust the track's position in the stereo field by dragging the Pan slider to the left and right; note how the sound moves between your speakers or headphones.

Two other important controls are Mute and Solo. Mute turns off the track's playback, whereas Solo turns off every track *except* the track that's soloed (Cubase SX lets you solo groups of tracks as well). Solo is especially useful when you're editing and applying EQ and effects to an individual channel while bringing it in and out of the full mix.

A Detailed View

In order to keep the screen uncluttered, Cubase SX at times hides parameters such as EQ, Inserts, and Sends. To invoke them at any time, click the corresponding buttons in the Track Mixer or Inspector. Figure 5-3 shows the Inspector with the EQ open.

Figure 5-3
Switching to the Inspector display to show the Bass track's EQ settings

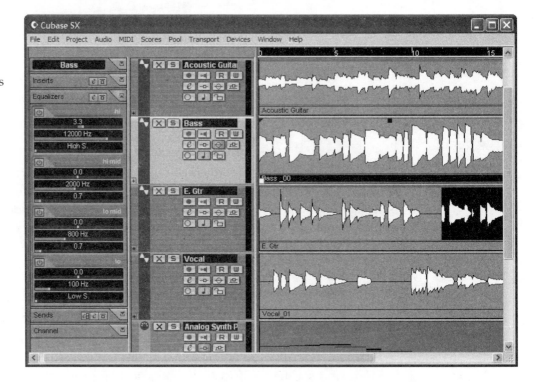

Figure 5-4 shows the same channel's EQ in the Track Mixer.

Figure 5-4
The Track Mixer shows the equalizer for four audio channels, after I click the Show Equalizers as Dials button.

If you want to see all the controls for a single channel, you can open the Channel Settings window shown in Figure 5-5 by clicking the E button next to the fader.

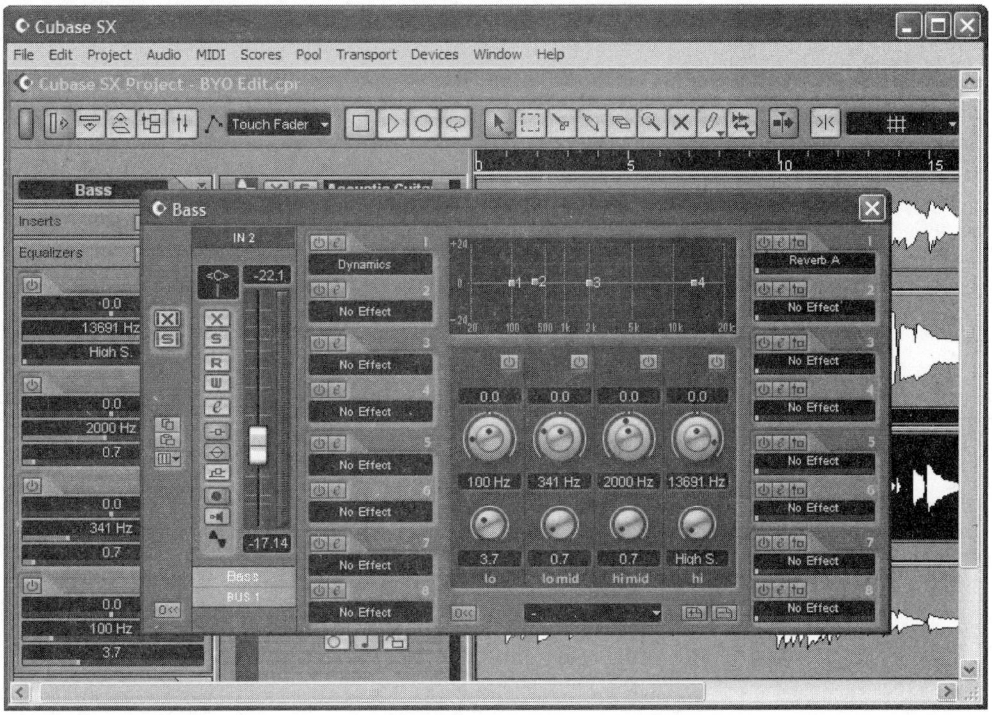

Figure 5-5
The VST Channel Settings window shows all the mix controls for one channel.

Step 2: Add EQ

Now that we've looked at the EQ in its many splendid forms, it's time to apply it to a track. I like to do this in the Channel edit window because it lets me change the EQ graphically and see how my settings affect the channel's overall tonal balance or color.

As the track plays, use the mouse to adjust the frequency, bandwidth, and boost/cut of each band, either by turning the knobs or by grabbing and dragging in the EQ Curve display above them (you can use your control surface to do this as well). You can toggle individual bands on and off, or you can bypass the EQ completely. In Figure 5-6, I've boosted the Bass track at 200 Hz (with a very narrow bandwidth) and rolled off the high frequencies (starting at around 6000 Hz). The Bass track will now sound dark and boomy.

Figure 5-6
I've adjusted the EQ for the Bass track. The knobs' settings are reflected in the EQ Curve display.

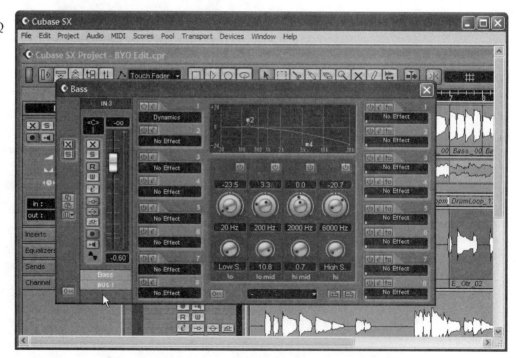

Effects and Processing

Cubase SX lets you choose from a wide array of audio effects to enhance your tracks. These can be applied in three ways:

❑ **As channel inserts** The effect is added to one channel at a time, and it affects only that channel.

❏ **As effects sends**   The effect can be applied to multiple channels simultaneously.

❏ **As a file-based operation**   The effect is applied directly to the audio data. (We'll cover this in Step 10: Add File-Based Effects.)

5 MINUTES

Step 3: Add an Insert Effect

When you apply an effect to an insert, the channel is routed through the effects (also known as *serial routing*, because the effect is applied inline). To demonstrate the adding of an insert effect, stay in the Channel edit window and follow these steps:

1. Move the mouse to an empty Insert Effects pane, to the left of the EQ section.

2. Click the pane to open a pop-up menu. You'll see all the effects available on the system (see Figure 5-7). I've selected Dynamics, a volume-control tool that will help keep the entire Bass track at a consistent level.

Figure 5-7
Clicking an Insert pane in the Channel edit window opens a pop-up menu showing all the available VST effects.

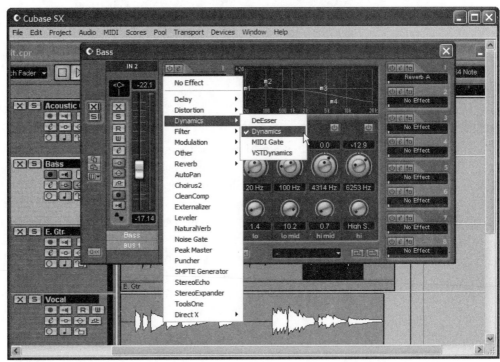

3. The Dynamics edit window opens automatically (see Figure 5-8). From here, you can load a preset or set the controls manually (and save the setting, if you like) while the music plays.

Figure 5-8
The Dynamics
window

Maximizing Your CPU Power

You can add several insert effects to a channel, though every effect you use is a drain on CPU resources. As a way to win back processor headroom, you can perform a file-based operation that "prints" the effect(s) to the audio file. Use the File | Export Audio menu (discussed in more depth in Step 13: Bounce Your Final Mix to Disk) to bounce the file to disk. Just be sure to solo the track you want to bounce; otherwise, Cubase SX will record the entire mix. You can then replace the dry file with the bounced version and disable the inserts. The computer is no longer using processing power to provide the effect live, or "on the fly." The effect is now part of the audio file itself and requires no more CPU power for playback than the same file without processing.

10 MINUTES

Step 4: Add a Send Effect

Whereas insert effects are placed in *series* on a single channel, send effects work in *parallel* on several channels. Sends are most commonly used for reverb and delay, effects that sound best when only a fraction of the effected (wet) signal is mixed with the original (dry) signal.

To add a send effect, follow these steps:

1. Open the Devices menu and choose VST Send Effects. The VST Send Effects window will open (see Figure 5-9).

Figure 5-9
The VST Send Effects Window

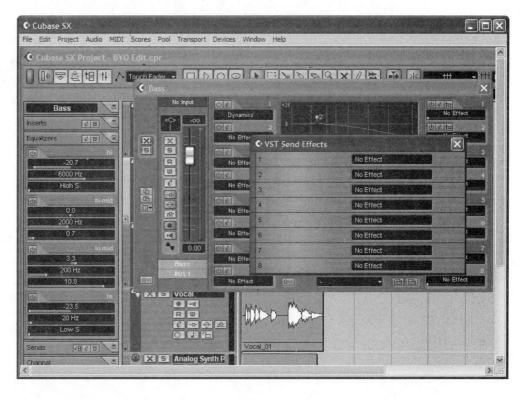

2. Click the top pane marked No Effect. A pop-up menu will appear (refer to Figure 5-7).

3. Scroll to Reverb | Reverb A. An edit window appears, as shown in Figure 5-10. I've recalled the "Large" preset and set the Dry/Wet balance to 100% Wet.

Figure 5-10
The Reverb A Edit
window. Note the
Dry/Wet mix slider
to the right.

4. Return to the Channel edit window. Reverb A is assigned to Send 1 (see Figure 5-11).

Figure 5-11
The Channel
edit window
with Send 1
assigned to
Reverb A
(upper right).
Send is turned
on (its button
is lit) and the
level slider is
at about 30
percent.

5. Activate the send. Use the slider under in the effects slot to adjust the level of the effect. You can increase the reverb applied to the track by moving the slider to the right.

If I open the Acoustic Guitar track—or any other track—Reverb A will appear in the Send 1 slot (see Figure 5-12). This is convenient because you'll often apply the same send effect to many channels.

Figure 5-12
The Channel edit window for the Acoustic Guitar track. As with the Bass track, Reverb A is assigned to Send 1.

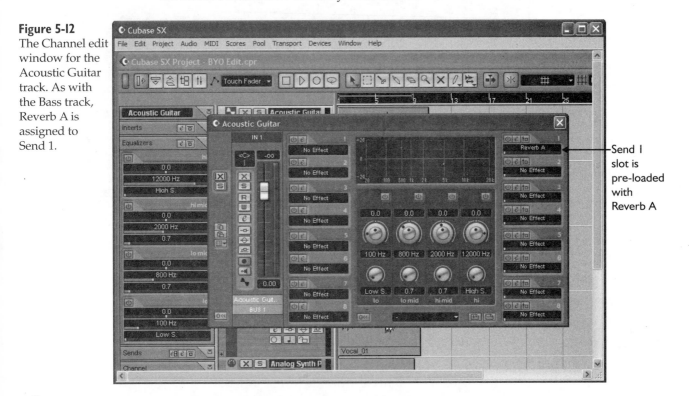

Send 1 slot is pre-loaded with Reverb A

Step 5: Mix MIDI Tracks

5 MINUTES

Cubase SX also lets you control MIDI parameters from its mixer. You can insert processors that affect MIDI playback (such as the Quantizer, which adjusts the notes' timing so they fall exactly on certain parts of the beat) or access MIDI effects via Sends—just like you do with audio. Figure 5-13 shows the Inspector and Channel edit window for a MIDI track.

Figure 5-13
The Inspector shows the Analog Synth Pad track's channel fader, whereas the Channel edit window also shows Insert and Send assignments. The Quantizer processor is open (top right).

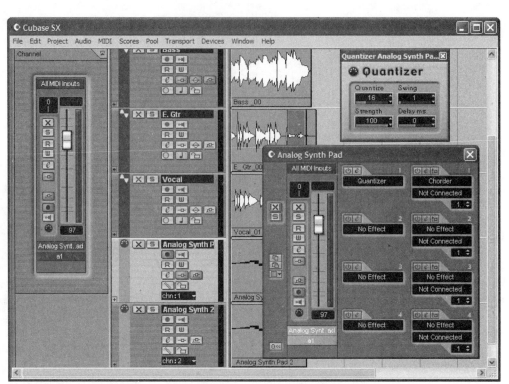

Assigning Multiple MIDI Tracks to a Single VSTi

When you're using a VSTi such as the A1, Cubase SX creates an *audio* channel for the instrument. This is separate from the MIDI track(s) assigned to that instrument, which contains only the performance data, but provides no audio in themselves. A single VSTi can receive data from more than one MIDI track at a time, each with its own MIDI effects settings. These will not change the *audio* settings of the VSTi.

5 MINUTES

Step 6: Add Master Effects

The master bus is the final stage in the mixer's signal path. This is where you set the overall output of your mix and add master effects, which process *all* the signals going through the mixer.

The master fader is available in the Track Mixer window (see Figure 5-14). You can also open the master bus via the Devices menu by selecting VST Devices | Outputs and Devices | Master Effects.

Figure 5-14
The Track Mixer with the master fader shown on the right

Master effects are especially useful for controlling the overall tonal balance and dynamics of a project. Figure 5-15 shows the VST Master Effects window with two effects enabled. The Puncher, which gives the music a more aggressive sound, is assigned before the master gain, whereas the Leveler is post-gain, where it can prevent the signal from overloading.

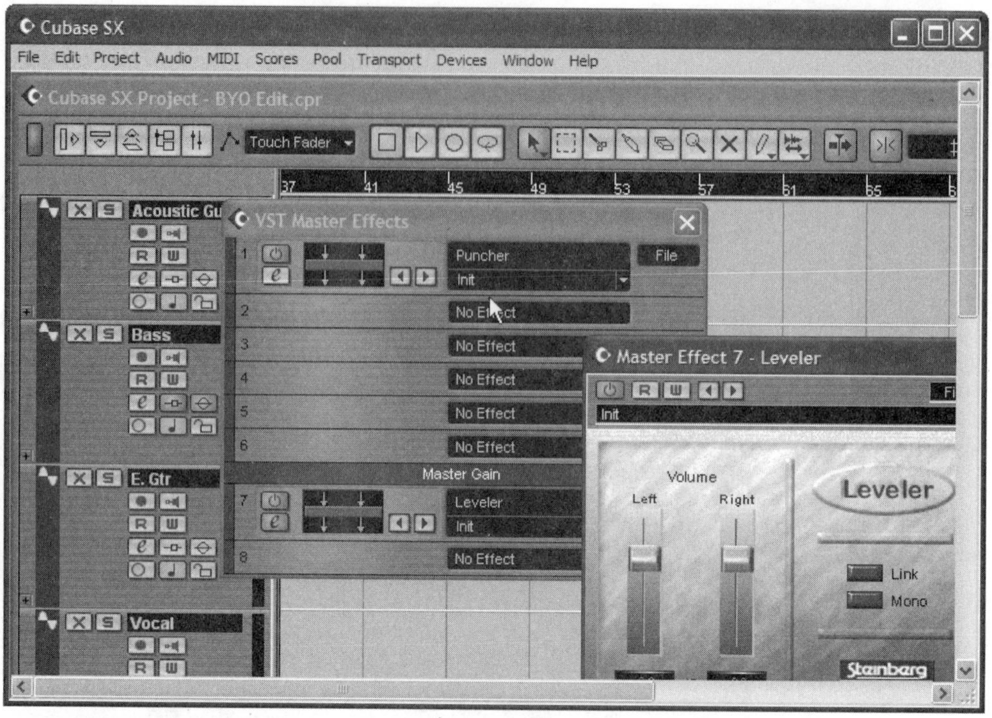

Figure 5-15
The VST Master Effects window, showing the Puncher (a pre-gain effect to tighten up the sound) and the Leveler (a post-gain effect that ensures against signal overload)

10 MINUTES

Step 7: Automate Your Mix

Setting up a mix can be as simple as positioning the faders and leaving them in place (called "set and forget"), but often a mix will require you to change the settings as the song plays. Typically this involves moving the volume faders to balance the song, and a mix is made more dynamic when this is done "on the fly." Cubase SX's *automation* records your moves and plays them back exactly. What's more, you can rerecord just your mixer moves as well as edit and punch in and out, just as you would when recording audio.

Let's say, for example, that the "BYOGW" Bass track comes in a little early and sustains for a little too long. Instead of rerecording it, I can use the mix automation to fix the problem. Here's how to do it:

1. Access the Bass track's mixer controls. (You can use the Track Mixer, Inspector, or Channel edit window. I've chosen the Inspector.)

2. Put the channel into Write automation by clicking the W button next to the fader (see Figure 5-16).

Figure 5-16
Pressing the "W"
button activates the
write automation
feature, which will
play back your
moves.

Write automation

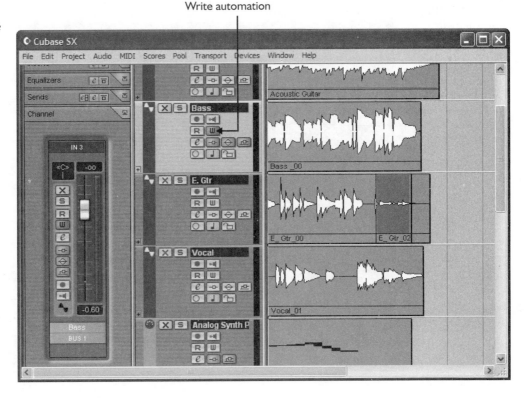

3. Mute the bass for the first four measures by pressing the mute-control X button next to the fader.

4. Begin playback (the Bass track is silent). If you hit the mute control again at the beginning of the second measure, you'll hear the bass return to the mix.

5. As the track continues to play, grab the fader and move it along with the music. As the Bass track comes to an end, slide the fader down gradually to create a fadeout.

6. Stop playback, disable Write automation for the channel, and, if it's not already lit, switch on Read automation by clicking the R button next to the fader (see Figure 5-17).

Figure 5-17
Pressing the "R" button activates the Read automation feature, which will record your moves.

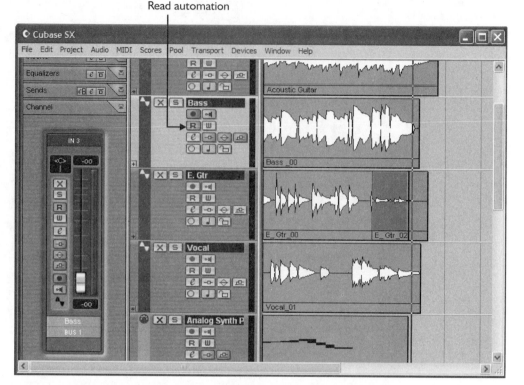

Read automation

When you hit play, the fader and mute controls will follow along, just as you entered them on the last run-through, with the Write function activated. If you want to make changes, you have two options. You can enable Write (with Read still active) and update the automation using the faders, or you can edit the automation using graphic tools by following these steps:

1. Go to the Bass track in the Track List and click the plus sign (+) at the bottom left of the track. The track will expand to show the automation subtracks (see Figure 5-18).

2. Select the Pencil tool from the toolbar and draw some new automation data. I've created a much longer fadeout for the Bass track in the Volume automation subtrack (see Figure 5-19).

3. Start playback. Now the fade is longer and more gradual.

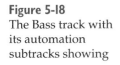

Figure 5-18
The Bass track with its automation subtracks showing

Figure 5-19
The Bass track with a new, longer fadeout drawn in

The Advantages of Graphical Editing

You can bypass the faders and go straight to graphical automation if you
wish by opening up the automation subtrack, selecting a parameter in the
pull-down menu, and drawing in automation data. Some automation
tasks are easier to perform graphically. For example, it would be very hard
to perform a gradual fadeout over 30 seconds with perfect evenness. But
set the zoom to show a 30-second interval in the Project window, grab the
Pencil tool, draw a straight, descending 45-degree line between the two
points, and—voilà—a perfectly linear 30-second fadeout.

Editing Your Work

So far, we've looked at PC-based recording tools that are similar to those you'd
find in a more traditional hardware environment. The element that sets the PC
apart from a conventional record-and-mix system is the way it lets you edit your
work after you've recorded it.

Cubase SX is replete with powerful editing tools, and many are suited for different environments (arranging, waveform editing, etc.). You've already seen
how to draw automation data with the Pencil tool, for example, but the Pencil
tool is also used in MIDI and audio editing. Instead of going through the tools
one by one, let's take a hands-on look at some typical editing jobs.

Step 8: Arrange Parts

Cubase SX lets you nondestructively rearrange parts after they've been recorded.
The applications for this technique are nearly limitless—everything from building
a new song out of old musical parts to replacing a bad note with a better one from
elsewhere in the recording. We'll arrange a new part and edit the transitions in the
following steps.

Editing Techniques for Both MIDI and Audio

*Many of the arranging techniques described in this section apply to MIDI as well as audio.
Experiment to see how they apply in both a MIDI and audio context, even if only one format
is described in the example.*

1. In the Project window, select the Zoom tool and drag it over the Bass track, zooming in around measure 5 (see Figure 5-20).

Figure 5-20
Zooming in on the Bass track

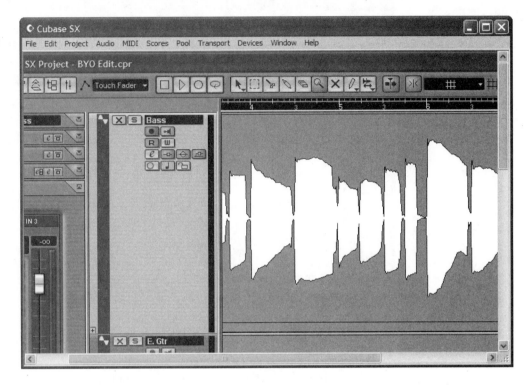

Cubase SX's Anywhere, Anytime Toolbox

Right-clicking your mouse will call up tools and the appropriate edit menus, no matter where you are in Cubase SX. These tools and menus are referred to as *context sensitive*.

2. In the toolbar, set the Snap mode to Grid with a value of Bar, and select the Split tool (the scissors icon), as shown in Figure 5-21.

3. With the Split tool selected, click on the Bass track at measure 5. The track will split into two separate events.

Figure 5-21
Setting the snap
mode to Grid
and selecting the
Split tool

Split tool   Snap mode to grid

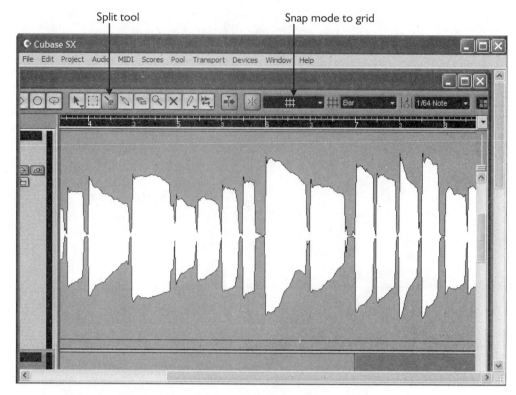

4. Split the Bass track again, at measure 6. We've now created an event
   with a duration of one measure (see Figure 5-22).

Figure 5-22
By splitting the Bass
track, we've created
a new event with
a duration of one
measure (center).

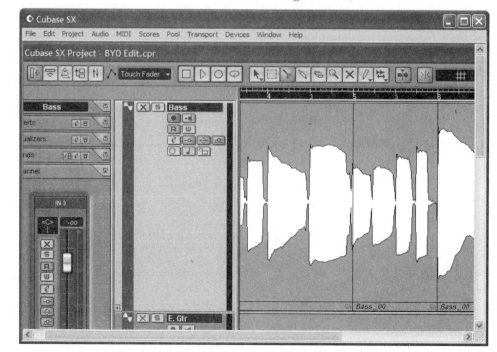

5. Choose the Erase tool and click the event we created between measures 5 and 6. It disappears, as shown in Figure 5-23.

Figure 5-23
Erasing an event on the Bass track

6. Navigate to measure 7 and use the Split tool to create an event that begins on measure 7 and ends on measure 8 (see Figure 5-24).

Figure 5-24
I've created an event between measures 7 and 8.

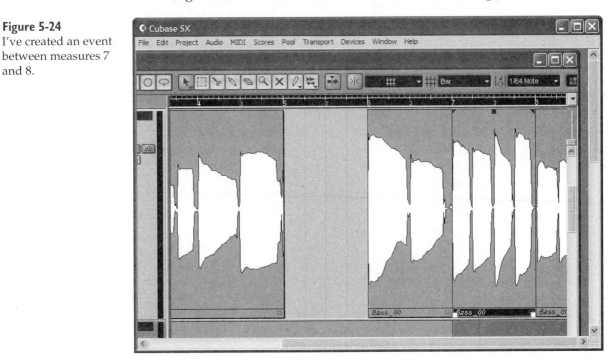

7. Activate the Object Selection tool and, while holding down ALT on the computer keyboard, drag the event over to measure 5. This places a *copy* at measure 5 without removing the event between measures 7 and 8 (see Figure 5-25).

Figure 5-25
The event created between measures 7 and 8 in step 6 is copied to fill the gap at measure 5.

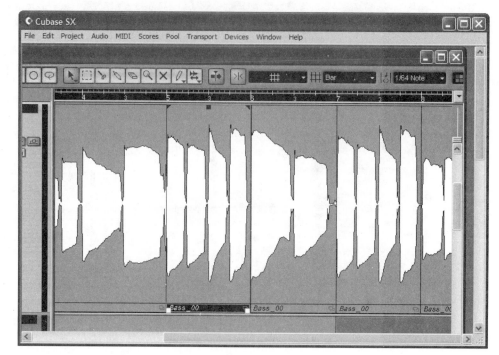

Smoothing Transitions

Now that I've rearranged the bass part, I'm hearing some awkwardness in the transition between the old and new parts. To fix this, I'll need to have finer control over the tools, so I disable Snap mode in the toolbar. Now, my moves aren't restricted to any set value.

If you look closely at the area around measure 5, you can see an abrupt splice in the waveform, which causes the Bass track to sound cut off. There are several ways to fix this, but I'll pick the simplest. Here are the steps for smoothing the transition:

1. With the Object Section tool, click the event preceding measure 5 (see Figure 5-26).

Figure 5-26
Selecting the event
leading up to the
editing splice.

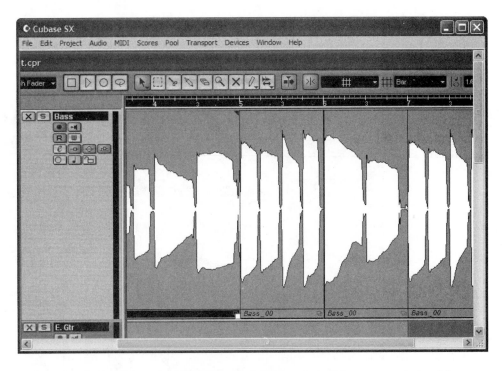

2. Place the cursor at the bottom-right corner of the event. A double arrow
   will appear. Click the corner and drag the cursor to the left, trimming
   the event by about a 16th note (see Figure 5-27).

Figure 5-27
Trimming an event
by dragging its
boundary

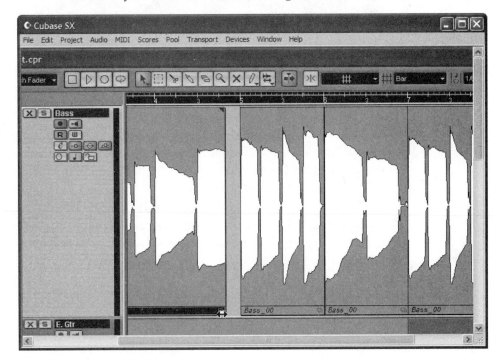

3. The event is shorter, but it still sounds cut off. Creating a fade will make the transition smoother. Click the Fade handle at the upper-right corner of the event and drag it to the left. Note how the waveform display changes to reflect the fadeout (see Figure 5-28).

Figure 5-28
Drawing a fadeout with the graphical editing tools in Cubase SX.

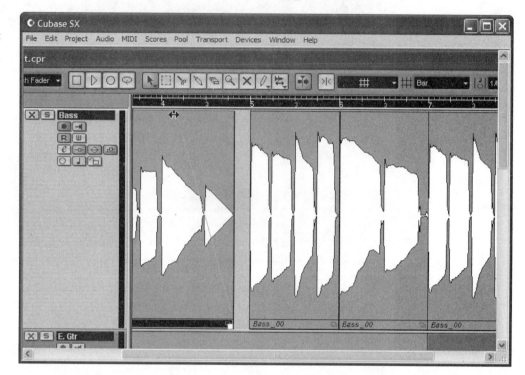

5 MINUTES

Step 9: Composite Virtual Tracks

When you record multiple takes of a track, as we did with the acoustic guitar back in Chapter 4, Cubase SX creates a new event for each take. I often like to use individual sections of the different takes to build a final part. This is known as *compositing*, and it's a valuable studio trick. Cubase SX makes it easy to manage these various takes by grouping them together into a *part*. Like an event, a part is visible in the Project window.

To create a part, select the track and, from the Edit menu, choose Select | All on Selected Tracks. Next, go to the Audio menu and choose Events to Part. Cubase SX creates a part that includes all the audio events on the current track, as shown in Figure 5-29.

Figure 5-29
The Acoustic Guitar part consists of several overlapping events.

When you double-click a part, Cubase opens the Part Editor (see Figure 5-30). As you can see, both the Acoustic Guitar_00 and Acoustic Guitar_01 events are visible.

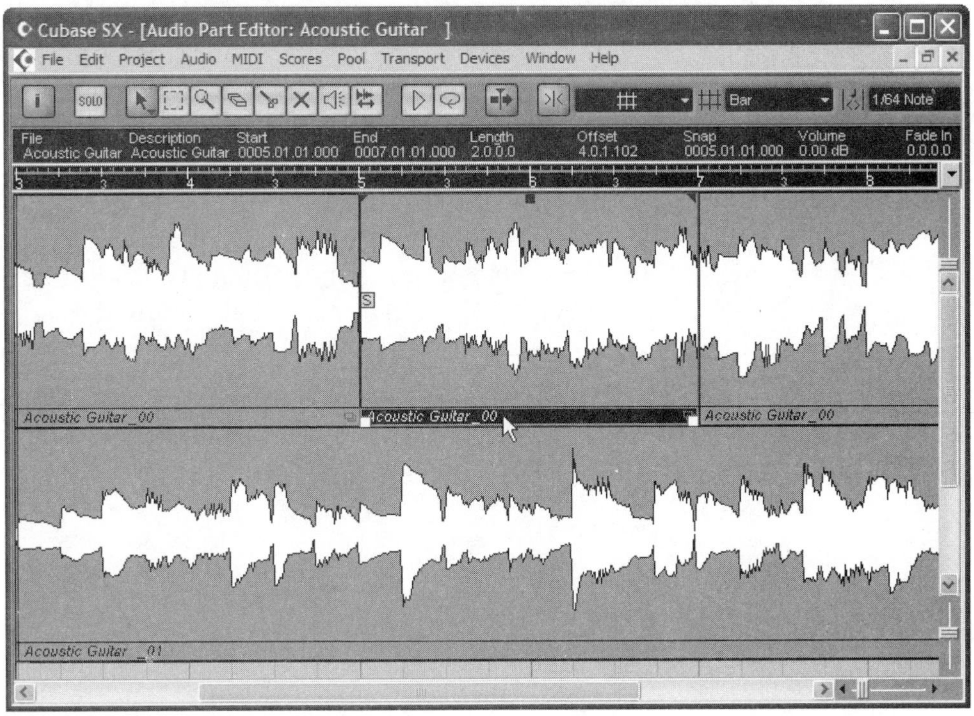

Figure 5-30
The Part Editor for the Acoustic Guitar part shows events from two separate audio files.

On playback, Cubase SX gives priority to the lowermost event (in this case, Acoustic Guitar_01). However, I'd like to use a portion of Acoustic Guitar_00. I'm going to split a portion of Acoustic Guitar_00 and drag it down to the lower lane in the Part Editor, as shown in Figure 5-31. When the song reaches measure 5, the newly extracted section of Acoustic Guitar_00 will play. When that event ends, Cubase SX will again play Acoustic Guitar_01.

Figure 5-31
A section of Acoustic Guitar_00 placed in the lower lane of the Part Editor

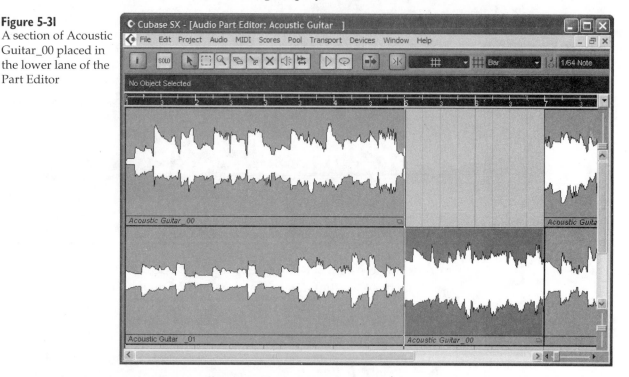

Listening to Individual Events

When you're dealing with multiple events, it's useful to be able to hear one at a time. Cubase SX lets you mute individual events without erasing them. This way, you can audition different parts that occupy the same section of a single track. In Figure 5-32, I've used the Mute tool to mute the rightmost section of Acoustic Guitar_01. Acoustic Guitar_00 will now play.

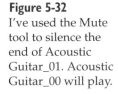

Figure 5-32
I've used the Mute tool to silence the end of Acoustic Guitar_01. Acoustic Guitar_00 will play.

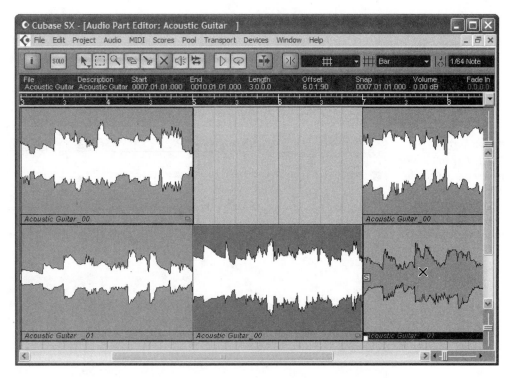

Muting Within the Project Window

You can also mute individual events and parts in the Project window—a more efficient alternative to using the Track Mixer's Mute control in some situations.

You can also audition individual events with the Play and Scrub tools, found in the Tool Palette or accessed by right-clicking over an event.

5 MINUTES

Step 10: Add File-based Effects

In addition to chopping up and repositioning your events nondestructively, Cubase SX lets you apply effects and other processors on the file level, which is known as *destructive editing* (a funny name for permanently altering the data—

as if it's a bad thing). This technique permanently alters the file (though Cubase SX can keep a copy of the original on hand for safekeeping). You can apply any VST and DirectX effects installed on your system (the same ones available in the Track Mixer) as well as use a number of audio utilities accessible only as file operations.

In Figure 5-33, you can see that E_Gtr_02 is a little low in level compared to E_Gtr_00. Balancing the two regions with the Track Mixer would be tricky.

Figure 5-33
The E. Gtr track with two separate events. The waveform display indicates that E_Gtr_02 is much quieter than E_Gtr_00.

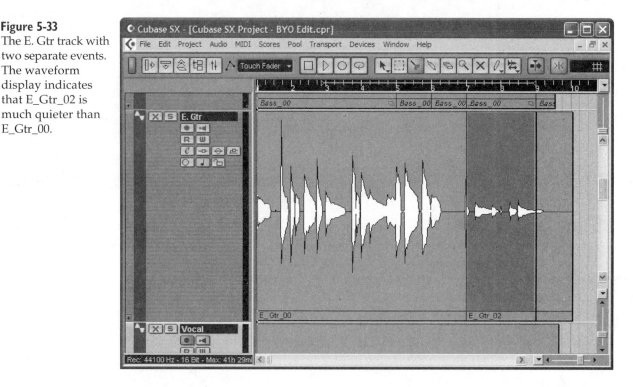

We can raise the gain of E_Gtr_02 with a file-based operation. Here's how:

1. Select the region in the Project window (this technique also works in the Part Editor).

2. Go to the Audio menu and choose Process | Gain (see Figure 5-34).

3. In the Gain window, enter the amount of change, positive or negative. In this case, I started out with a 6 dB boost, and, finding the event still too quiet, went back and added another 8 dB. The result can be seen in Figure 5-35.

Editing, Mixing, and Processing Your Music   **139**

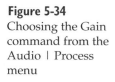

Figure 5-34
Choosing the Gain
command from the
Audio | Process
menu

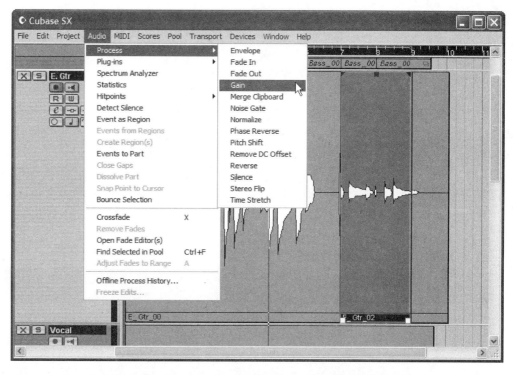

Figure 5-35
After the gain
change, E_Gtr_02
is a much better
match for E_Gtr_00.

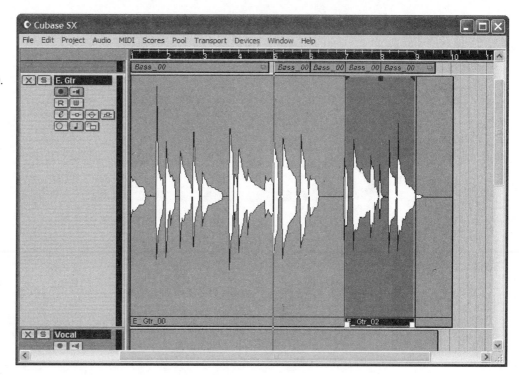

Checking Your Edits Before Committing

Cubase SX lets you preview your work before applying a file-based operation. Also, you can always "undo" your operations (CTRL-Z) if you don't like the results.

Step 11: Micro-edit Your Files

Although you can accomplish almost all your edits directly in the Project and Part Editor windows, there are times when you need the greater precision offered by the individual audio and MIDI editors.

The Sample Editor

The Sample Editor gives you a detailed view of audio events and files, and it allows you to perform a number of file-based operations. It can zoom all the way in to the sample level (at 44.1 kHz, there are 44,100 samples per *second*, so that's pretty darn precise).

Here's how to use the Sample Editor to permanently silence a section of E_Gtr_02:

1. Open the Sample Editor by double-clicking the E_Gtr_02 region (see Figure 5-36).

Figure 5-36
The Sample Editor
for E_Gtr_02

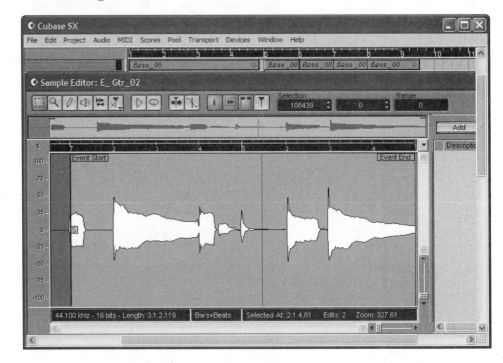

2. Use the Range Selection tool (the square) to select a portion of the file (see Figure 5-37).

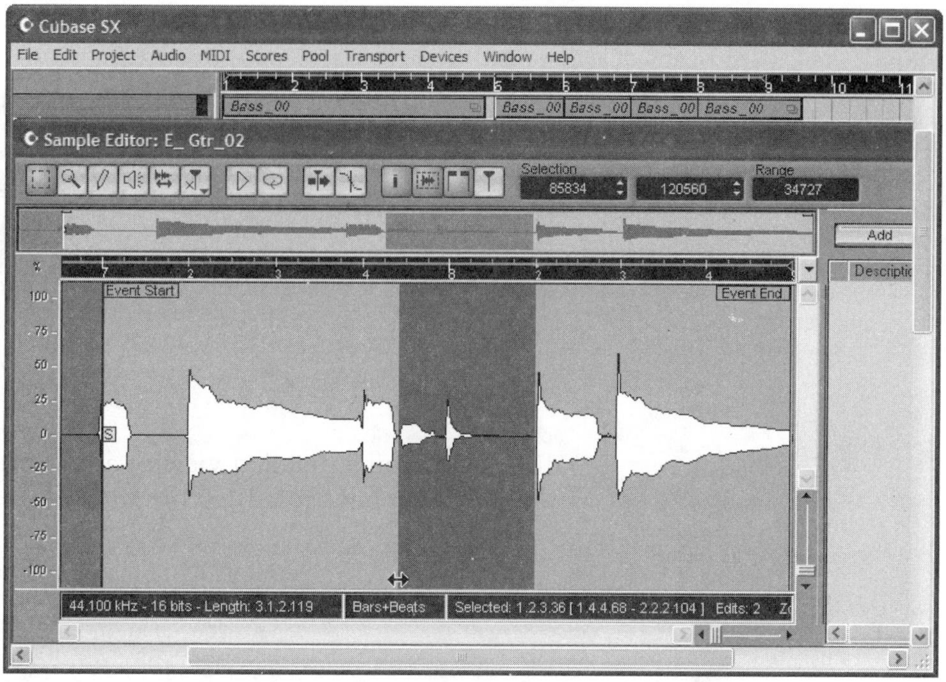

Figure 5-37
A portion of the region for is selected for editing.

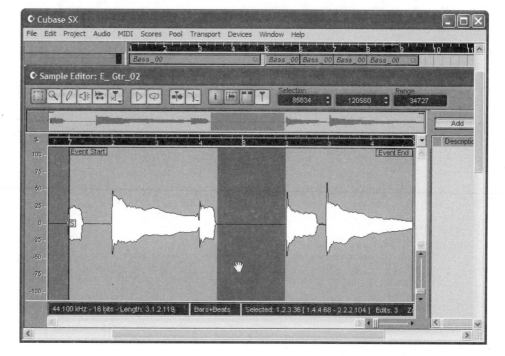

3. In the Audio menu, select Process | Silence. The selected area will be permanently silenced (see Figure 5-38).

Figure 5-38
The selected area has been silenced. The rest of the file is unaffected.

The MIDI Editors

Cubase SX has a number of MIDI editors that let you alter MIDI events on an individual basis. These editors include the Event List, the Score Editor, and the graphical Drum and Key Editor (see Figure 5-39).

Figure 5-39
The Key Editor for the Analog Synth Pad. Each bar represents a single note.

As an example, I can use the Key Editor to lower the pitch of the first note shown in Figure 5-39 by dragging it down an octave with the mouse (see Figure 5-40).

You can use the Key Editor to enter new notes, erase individual notes, change the length or start position of notes, and more. You can even edit controller data, such as pitch bend and modulation (see Figure 5-41).

Figure 5-40
Using the Key
Editor, I've
transposed a
note from C4 to
C3—down one
octave.

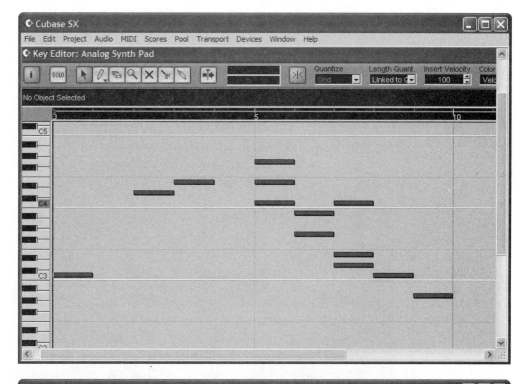

Figure 5-41
Modulation data
in the Key Editor's
Controller pane

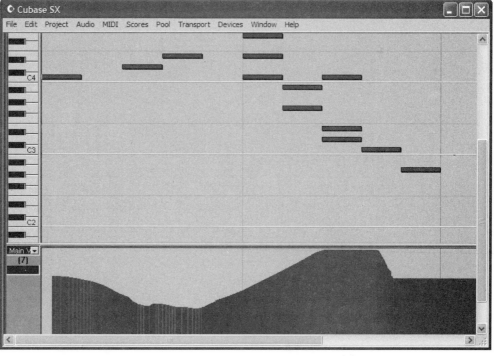

10 MINUTES

Step 12: Time-stretch an Imported File

In Chapter 4 we imported a stereo audio file into an existing arrangement. Although this is a powerful tool, there are times when the file you want to import does not match the tempo of your project.

For example, I've imported a two-bar drum loop into the "BYOGW" song. Unfortunately, its tempo is 130 beats per minute—10 bpm faster than my project's tempo, which makes it two bars too short for my arrangement's two bars. However, I can stretch the loop to fit by changing the Object Selection tool to the Sizing Applies Time Stretch option, as shown in Figure 5-42.

Figure 5-42
The Object Selection tool with the Sizing Applies Time Stretch option active

Now when I drag the boundaries of the drum loop so that the event encompasses two bars (see Figure 5-43), Cubase SX changes the duration of the audio file to exactly two bars, and the loop will now play in sync with the rest of my track.

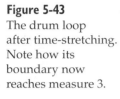

Figure 5-43
The drum loop
after time-stretching.
Note how its
boundary now
reaches measure 3.

I can use Cubase SX's Edit | Repeat command to quickly copy and paste the
loop so that it plays for the duration of my song (see Figure 5-44).

Figure 5-44
Cubase SX's Repeat
command can fill
out the song with
the drum loop.

Step 13: Bounce Your Final Mix to Disk

Once your edits are in place and you've automated your mix, you're ready to create a final mixdown. Cubase SX can export a stereo audio file that contains all your automation and effects. To bounce your project down to a stereo file, follow these steps:

1. Set the Left and Right locators to include the part of your project you wish to export (in this case, the entire song).

2. Place all automated tracks into Read mode.

3. Open the File | Export | Audio menu and choose Audio Mixdown.

4. The Audio Mixdown window appears (see Figure 5-45). Check the options to include automation and effects in your mix.

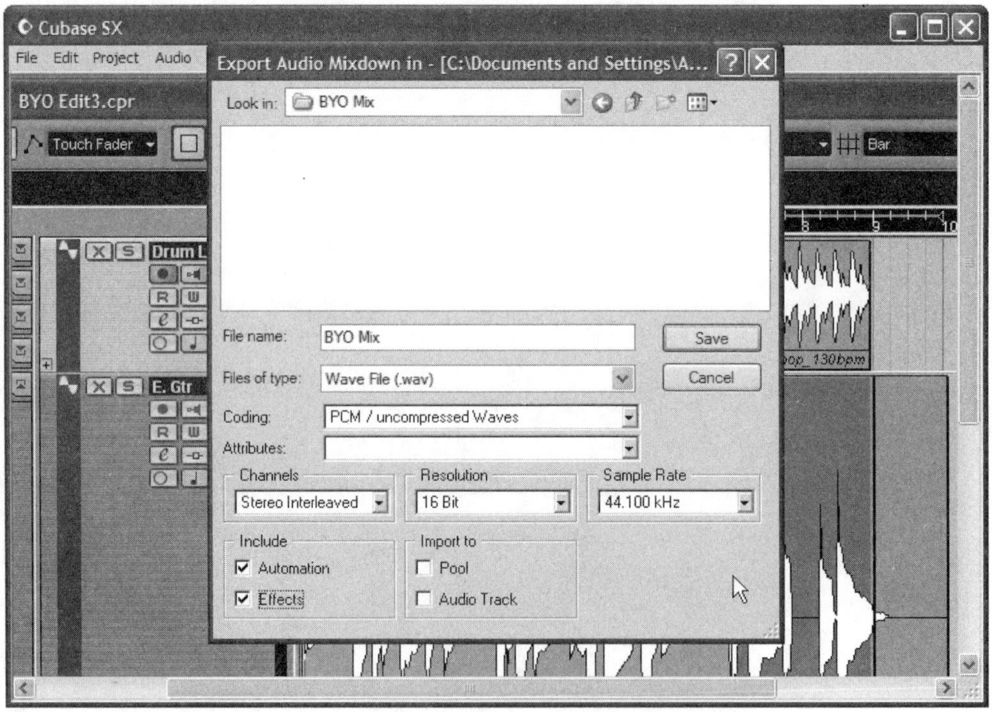

Figure 5-45
The Audio Mixdown window with the desired options for a mixdown selected

5. Uncheck the options to import the bounced track to the Pool and Audio Track (these options can be used for bouncing a submix, but we'll ignore them here).

6. Choose the resolution, sample rate, and format of the file. Because we're going to burn this file onto a CD, choose a stereo, interleaved WAV file at 16 bit, 44.1 kHz.

7. Name the file and click Save.

Congratulations! You've just created a final stereo mixdown of your project, complete with all your edits, mix moves, and effects.

Moving On

Chapter 6 deals with preparing a finished mixdown for mastering. Mastering is the final stage before your work is distributed over the Internet and on CD. You'll be relieved to know that the hard work is all behind you (at least from a conceptual point of view). Producing music worthy of public consumption is the most demanding task, both creatively and technically. But now that this stage is complete, turning your mixdowns into MP3s and professionally packaged CDs is just plain fun!

At this point you should have completed the following tasks:

❏ Set levels and EQ'd individual tracks in your project

❏ Added an insert and a send effect

❏ Recorded and edited automation moves on your mixdown

❏ Composited virtual tracks

❏ Copied and pasted existing parts into other parts of the arrangement

❏ Performed basic MIDI editing

❏ Time-stretched an imported audio file

❏ Bounced your project to disk

Chapter 6

Mastering, Burning, and Packaging Your CD

Tools of the Trade

CD-RW drive

Nero Burning ROM CD-burning software

Blank CD-R discs

Label templates

Mastering is the last step in preparing your music for CD, and it deals with finished stereo mixdown files. In professional recording, mastering is done at a separate facility with different equipment and different personnel. A mastering engineer is there to provide subtle touches in tonal balance and levels, to listen to the work as a whole, and to prepare the final product for mass production.

In our one-stop solution to music production, though, we'll tackle mastering with the same tools we used to record and mix: our trusty PC and audio-editing software. Because we're comfortable working with Cubase SX, we'll just make a psychological transition into mastering mode and perform any finishing touches with built-in EQ and plug-ins. By the time we reach the mastering stage, we just want a nice sheen on our work before burning it to CD.

Editing and Processing Your Files

Editing and processing are also done in the mixdown stage, but for mastering we're listening for different qualities. What was fine for a song by itself may not work in the company of other songs, so we'll address any context issues here. Following are some of the most common context-sensitive issues that arise in mastering.

10 MINUTES

Step 1: Trim the File Length

When you listen to the mixdown of a single song, you're probably not really aware of how long the *track* is. But when you start to assemble your songs on a CD, you don't want the silence at the beginning and end or your audio files to be too long or too short. So now's the time to go into your file and trim off excess space before the first note of music. Similarly, listen to the end of the song, where the last note fades from hearing. Then use your eyes to see how long the track plays in silence and imagine the exact moment you'd like the new track to begin.

If the track ends early, it means the next song will start too soon. If the track continues to play in silence, the gap between songs on the CD will be too long.

Trimming silence from the end of a track is easy. Following are the steps for importing a stereo mixdown into Cubase SX, where we'll shorten the file's total length:

1. Launch Cubase SX and select File | New Project | Stereo Mastering Setup.

2. Choose File | Import | Audio File and navigate to your song file.

3. Double-click the file and it will open up in track 1 of the project window. Double-click the waveform display in the Project window to open the Sample Editor window, as shown in Figure 6-1.

Figure 6-1
The Sample Editor allows you to make alterations to the audio waveform on the file level, which are permanent, as opposed to mixer settings, which are only temporary and not part of the actual audio file.

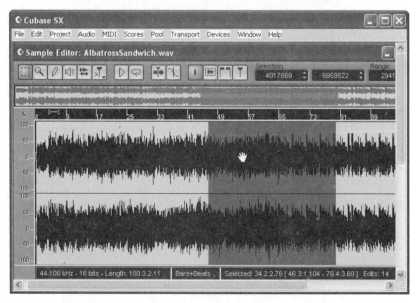

4. Scroll to the end of the track and use the horizontal slider to zoom in enough so that you can see some of the music and the very end of the track.

5. Audition the passage several times and decide how much silence you'd like to trim.

6. Use the cursor tool to highlight the area from the end of the file (the far right) to a point that's still in the silent area, as shown in Figure 6-2.

7. Press the DELETE key and audition the results. If you've deleted too much or too little, press CTRL-Z (or select Undo from the Edit menu) and try again.

Figure 6-2
Deleting silence at the end of a track. The highlighted section is ready to be removed from the file at the touch of the DELETE button.

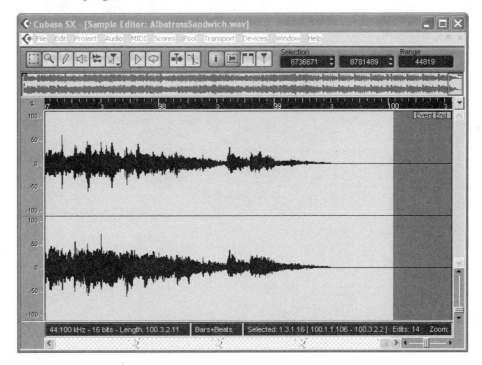

If by chance you have to *add* silence, follow the preceding steps, but instead of deleting a selected region of silence at step 7, *copy* it (CTRL-C). Place the cursor at the end of the file and then paste (CTRL-V). If that's too much silence, don't undo, but instead work from the end of the file and delete smaller sections of time.

10 MINUTES

Step 2: EQ Your Song

After you've lived with a tune's initial mixdown, you may decide that you want to change the tonal balance slightly. Rather than go back and redo the mix, you can apply a subtle change at the mastering stage. You can also decide to apply EQ after hearing other songs you intend to include on your CD. Sometimes an individual song that sounds good in isolation may be too bright or too dark in context with other tunes.

To EQ your file, open the Sample Editor by double-clicking the waveform display in the project window. Figure 6-3 shows a subtle EQ setting with a gradual slope, with the high and low ranges set to *shelving* rather than *parametric* settings.

Figure 6-3
Applying EQ at the mastering stage is best done subtly. In this case, we're adding a slight boost in the bass, a peak at the 2 KHz range, a dip at 5 KHz, and an overall boost at the 10 KHz range. This will give the song a little punch and sizzle without making it overly boomy or bright.

To make your EQ settings permanent, you must bounce to disk (see Chapter 5) because EQ settings are not made directly to the audio file but rather are incorporated as an option in the bounce-to-disk process.

Step 3: Compress Your File

Compressing is a very important mastering effect because it smoothes out uneven volume levels and yields a slick, punchy effect. Because compression targets higher volume levels, it allows you to turn up the volume overall without distortion. The result is that the quieter levels come up in volume, but the louder levels don't grow proportionately. If you picture this process represented graphically, it narrows, or *compresses,* the dynamic range, thus giving the effect its name.

You may have done some compressing in the mixdown stage, but it's appropriate in the mastering stage, too. As with EQ, compression at the mastering stage is best applied subtly.

To compress a file, import the stereo mixdown file as you did when trimming the file length. Open the Sample Editor and then follow these steps:

1. Place the cursor anywhere within the waveform display and press CTRL-A (Select All). Choose Audio | Plug-ins | Dynamics | Dynamics, as shown in Figure 6-4. This reveals the compression screen.

Figure 6-4
Access the compressor by selecting Dynamics from the choices in the Audio | Plug-ins menu.

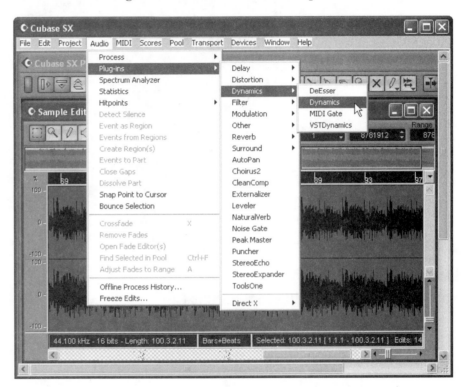

2. Vary the compressor's controls, as shown in Figure 6-5, but make your changes subtle. Don't use a ratio higher than about 4:1, and don't boost the overall level. You'll have another chance to adjust the volume. Use Preview to judge whether your work sounds better or worse than the original.

Figure 6-5
Compressing during
the mastering stage
should be done with
a light touch. Here,
the ratio is a very
reasonable 3.3:1.

![HEADS UP!]

Making Permanent Changes to the Audio File

*Compression is a file-based operation, which means it permanently alters the audio,
unlike effects applied with the mixer, which work in real time and can be changed at any
time without affecting the underlying audio file. If you're not sure you'll like the results,
create a copy of the file and work from that.*

3. When you hear an improvement in the song's smoothness, click
    Process. The changes will be made to the audio file immediately, as
    shown in Figure 6-6. No bouncing to disk is required here; the effect
    is "rendered in place."

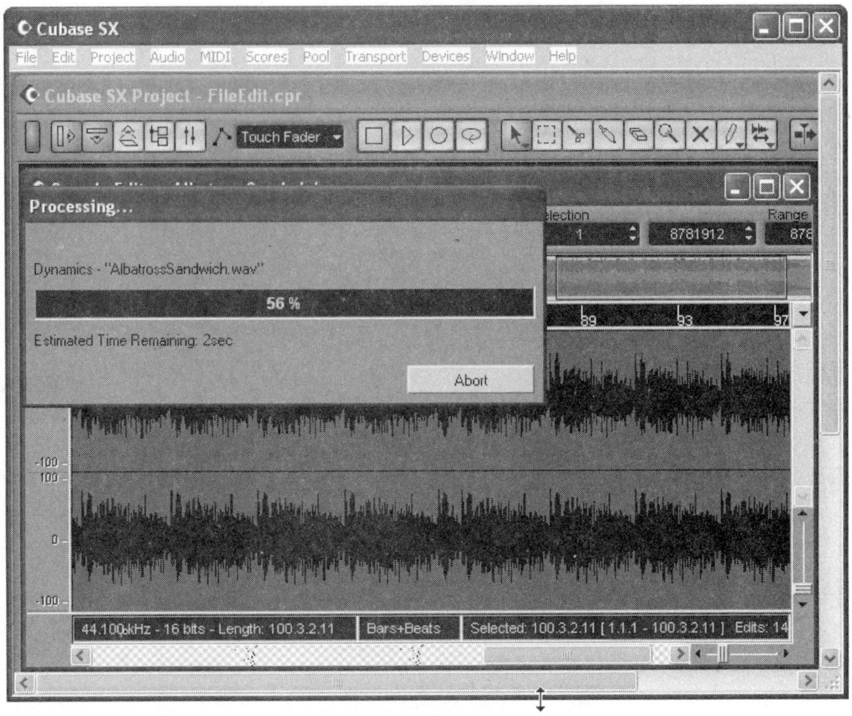

Figure 6-6
Unlike the bounce-to-disk process necessary to render EQ settings, compression is effected immediately in the file.

10 MINUTES

Step 4: Level-match and Normalize Your Song

Before you burn your CD, you should listen to your songs together and preferably in the order they'll appear on the CD. One of the most important qualities to listen for at this stage is the relative volume levels of the songs. No song should seem dramatically louder or softer than another. This is true whether the song is a sensitive ballad or a death-metal screamer.

If you decide a tune needs to come down in volume, just invoke the Gain tool in Audio Process. Following are the specific steps to reduce the overall volume level of a file:

1. After importing the mixdown file into an audio track in Cubase SX's Project window, double-click the waveform. This launches the Sample Editor.

2. Place the cursor anywhere in the waveform region and press CTRL-A (Select All).

3. Select Audio | Process | Gain, as shown in Figure 6-7. Any changes you make to the audio file from the Audio | Process menu will be permanent.

Figure 6-7
Selecting the Gain option from the Process menu allows you to make overall gain changes to a file.

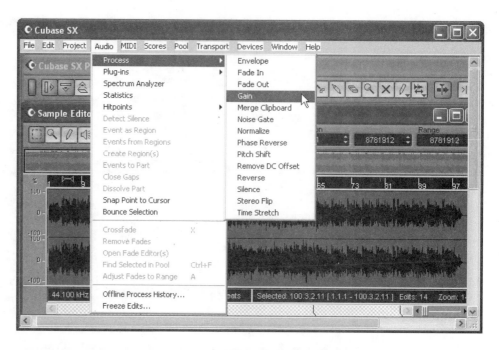

4. Move the slider to the left, making sure that negative numbers appear in the display, as shown in Figure 6-8. This will ensure a volume reduction.

Figure 6-8
The Gain parameters window allows you to boost or cut the volume of a file, but we're using it here to reduce a file that's too loud overall.

Boosting the volume is a little trickier, however, because just cranking the Gain lever to the right to produce positive numbers might cause distortion. Therefore, it's best to raise levels through a process called *normalization*, which raises the volume of a file without letting the loudest parts of it go into the red. Normalization can also be used to make multiple files reach the same peak levels without distorting.

Follow these steps to normalize your file:

1. After importing the mixdown file into an audio track in Cubase SX's Project window, double-click the waveform to launch the Sample Editor.

2. Place the cursor anywhere in the waveform region and press CTRL-A (Select All).

3. Select Audio | Process | Normalize, as shown in Figure 6-9. Remember, any changes you make will be permanent.

Figure 6-9
You can normalize all the way up to 100 percent, and values of 99 and 100 are the most common to take advantage of your system's maximum headroom (the area for optimum volume level before distortion occurs).

Checking for Rogue Peaks Before Normalizing

If your normalization efforts don't seem to make any difference, it could be you have a rogue peak—a high level that prevents the normalization process from being effective on the entire file. Eyeball your file in the Sample Editor for spikes and bring them down individually by highlighting each one with the cursor and applying gain reduction to only that portion of the audio. Then apply normalization and watch your file grow!

File Formats

When you work in Cubase SX or other audio programs, you're dealing with uncompressed audio that can be turned into an audio CD. But other formats take advantage of *compression*, a data reduction process that makes audio files smaller without sacrificing too much quality. (This is not to be confused with level compression, a dynamics operation that works on the volume of file.) The advantages of a smaller digital file outweigh the slight compromise in sound for many situations, such as music for the Web, where small files mean quicker downloading.

Now that we've got music files in a state of near completion, let's examine the file formats available, and their uses in music production.

WAV or AIF

Wave and Audio Interchange File Format, or AIFF (herein abbreviated to their three-letter extension designations WAV and AIF), are the Windows and Mac file formats that deal in uncompressed, linear audio at a 16-bit/44.1 kHz resolution. Only these two types of files can be made directly into audio CDs that play in a DiscMan, boom box, car stereo, or high-end home-entertainment CD deck.

All other file formats employ a form of data compression (not to be confused with audio compression, a dynamic process) and can't be made into audio CDs without being converted to WAV or AIF (or SD2, but that's rarely encountered by home recordists). When you create and edit audio in Cubase SX or any other professional recording application, you're dealing in the WAV and AIF formats. A CD burner will write any type of file (including WAV) to a CD as data, but to create an audio CD, the file format must be WAV or AIF.

10 MINUTES   Step 5: Convert to MP3

MP3 was the first successful audio-compression format that provided acceptable quality at about one tenth the size of a WAV or AIF file. It employs *lossy* compression, which permanently discards data that it deems audibly indiscernible to human ears. Unlike Zip compression, which restores a file to its original uncompressed state, data that undergoes lossy compression is irretrievably lost. But the sound quality in the MP3 compression scheme is quite good, and the savings in disk space and download time have made it a hit with the Web crowd.

In Cubase SX, converting your work to MP3, WMA, or RealAudio (QuickTime requires a separate encoder) is a simple process of exporting your audio from the File menu. I'll show the steps for converting to the MP3 format, but the process is similar for WMA and RealAudio.

To convert your stereo mixdown file (currently in WAV format) to MP3, perform the following steps:

1. With your desired mixdown file in a project window track, choose Open File | Export | Audio Mixdown, and you'll be presented with the screen shown in Figure 6-10. Click the Files of Type pull-down menu to see your available options.

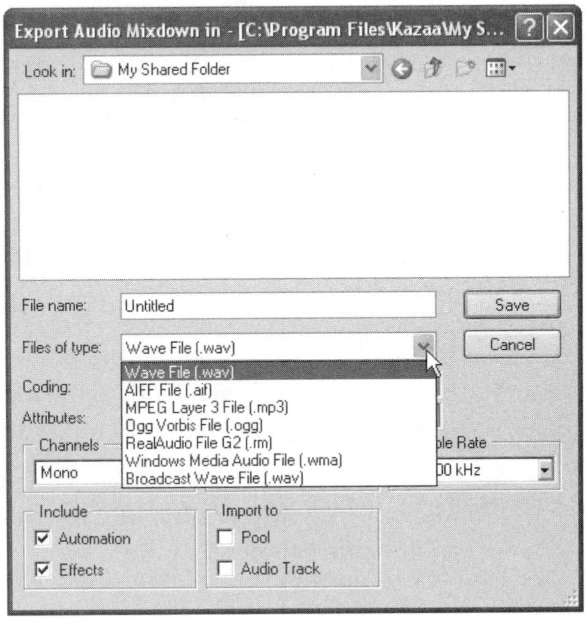

Figure 6-10
The options for exporting audio in Cubase are numerous and versatile.

2. Select MP3, and a new screen appears with parameters specific to the MP3 file format. Change the radio button in the Channels field to Stereo. Leave the Quality setting at Highest, and leave Automation and Effects checked in the Include field. Keep the setting of 44.100 kHz in the Sample Rate pull-down menu. Click the Attributes pull-down menu to reveal the options, as shown if Figure 6-11.

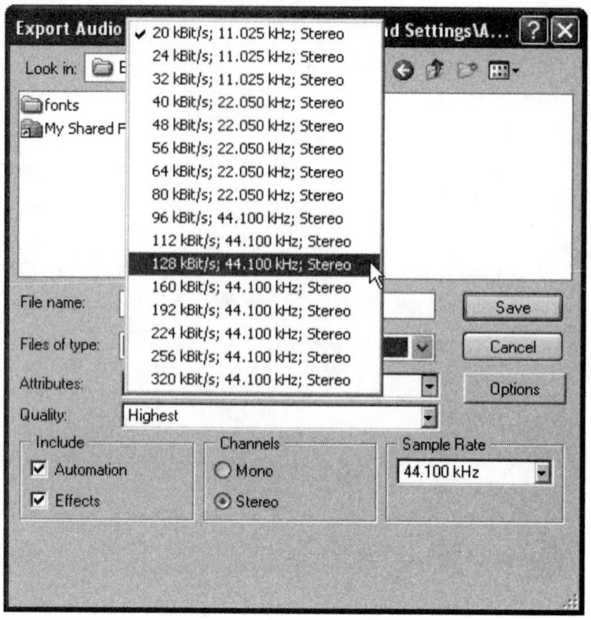

Figure 6-11
The Attributes window of the MP3 file format, with the option "128 kBit/s; 44.100 kHz; Stereo" highlighted with the cursor.

3. Choose the option "128 kBit/s; 44.100 kHz; Stereo."

4. Click the Options button and give your file some text attributes, if you like (this is optional).

5. Name the file and navigate to the location where you'd like your new files stored. Click Save and you're done. Well, almost (see step 6).

6. To test your newly created MP3 file, open it up on your favorite MP3 jukebox program or offload it to your favorite MP3 player and go for a jog while listening!

HEADS UP!

Fixing MP3 Problems in the Original File Format

If you hear a problem with your file, you'll have to go back to the original audio program, fix it, and then reexport a new file. It's much easier to fix MP3 files this way than to try to edit them in their MP3 format.

WMA

WMA is another lossy compression file format, developed by Microsoft, that rivals MP3. Its files are even smaller than MP3's, and at this writing, WMA is gaining popularity. It's difficult to make a qualitative judgment in the MP3-WMA rivalry, so if you're planning on creating music for the Web, you should encode your WAV files in both formats.

QuickTime

Developed by Apple Computer, QuickTime is a popular video format, but its audio engine is quite good, too, and has the distinct advantage of being able to stream as well as download. Although QuickTime is a popular audio and video player for the Mac, QuickTime for Windows is generally used in a video context.

RealAudio

RealNetworks' RealAudio is an *audio-streaming* format, which means the file doesn't need to download entirely onto your hard drive before it starts playing back. This offers two advantages: The file starts playing almost immediately, and you're not left with a huge file when the song completes because no data is being saved to your hard drive (except for a small "pointer" file that directs your browser to the file's server location). Streaming also allows the server to prevent you from having a permanent copy of the music, which can be an advantage—at least to the distributor.

Tape

Tape is a linear format, and you must write data to it in real time. This might make it seem quaint and inefficient in the age of random access, but tape still has its place.

Digital Audio Tape

A few years ago, DAT (Digital Audio Tape) was the mixdown medium of choice for home musicians. It has been supplanted by cheap CD recorders, but there are still plenty of DAT machines and DAT tapes around. And they still sound great! If you find you have to record a file to DAT, you can use the S/PDIF jacks on your interface and the DAT deck for a straight digital transfer, or you can record/play back through the analog jacks. The only disadvantage with using the analog ports is that you have to watch your levels.

Cassette and Other Analog Tape

I don't know about you, but as much as I loathe the cassette medium for its sonic deficiencies, I still have several cassette decks in my house (and tons of tapes) that I won't throw out. Cassettes still have a foothold in the marketplace, as do other analog tape media such as open-reel quarter-inch tape. When you record to cassette, you should highly compress your signal, enough so that it slams the tape as hard as possible without causing the cassette deck's record-level meter to go into the red (actually, it's okay if the short, loud peaks go into the red momentarily). This yields the best signal-to-noise ratio on a medium that's very narrow with respect to noise floor and headroom. A hot signal with a narrow dynamic range is best for recording to cassettes.

TIPS OF THE TRADE

Getting Optimal Results When Recording to Cassette Tape

When recording to cassette, use only high-bias tapes (which are, ironically, more expensive now than blank CDs) and employ Dolby C and HX noise-reduction circuitry (if available). A common practice is to record with every light below 0 on steadily and allow the red lights to flash for only a half second or so. This allows for the "hottest" transfers possible and usually yields no distortion—as long as the instances of going into the red are momentary.

Burning a CD, Step by Step

Burning a CD is the last step in the recording process, the one that produces the tangible results of your hard-won efforts. The good news is that it's also the *easiest* step in the sometimes long journey through the creative and technological wilderness. In short, burning a CD is a no-brainer! Let's get to it!

2 MINUTES

Step 6: Launch the Burning Software

The CD-RW drive that you bought probably came with software that allows you to burn both audio and data CDs. I've found that just about any software package that does both will do the job, but for this project I've chosen Ahead's Nero Burning ROM because of its ease of use and professional features. In particular, Nero Burning ROM includes a wizard and a simplified version of itself named Nero Express, so you never have to deal with the program's complexities if you don't want to. Just follow the cartoon icons on the wizard screens. Install the program from the CD-ROM like any other software and double-click the Nero Express icon. You'll be greeted with the screen in Figure 6-12, which is just about as self-explanatory as could be.

Figure 6-12
The opening screen to Nero Express offers all your options up front. No digging through menus.

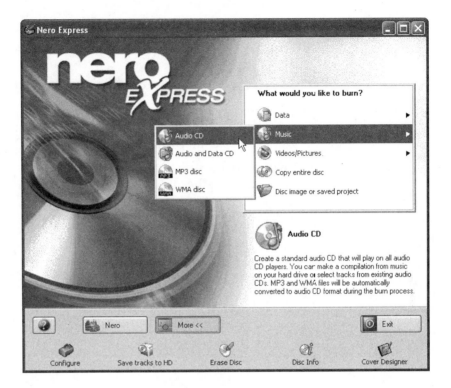

Audio or Data?

Before we begin to burn a CD, let's clear up one point about audio vs. data in the realm of CD semantics. An audio CD is one that plays music in a CD player. Everything else is data. Even burning MP3 files to a CD is creating a data disc. MP3 discs won't play in a CD player. Nero and other programs may present data and MP3 burning as separate functions, but that's just a courtesy to the user. MP3 files are plain data, and they have to be converted by the software residing in an MP3 player. For now, let's stick with burning an audio CD.

2 MINUTES

Step 7: Prepare Your Files

Before creating a CD, you have to have ready all the tracks destined for burning. It helps to store them all in a single folder, but you don't have to worry about their order yet. We'll wait until the files are in Nero to shift them around.

The files should be named with song titles rather than numbers, so that as you experiment with different orders (sequences) you'll be able to tell at a glance what songs are where. If all your files aren't in a single folder, place them all there now and rename them, if necessary, to conform to a uniform labeling scheme, because this is what will appear in the various windows of our CD-burning software.

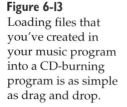

Step 8: Sequence and Assemble a Playlist

Importing audio files into Nero is simple: Just drag them from the desktop folder and drop them into Nero's open window. If you put all your songs in one folder, you can just select them all (CTRL-A), grab one of the selected files with the mouse, and drag them en masse into the Nero window, as shown in Figure 6-13. An even easier way is to just grab the folder, without opening it, and drop it in the window.

Figure 6-13
Loading files that you've created in your music program into a CD-burning program is as simple as drag and drop.

With the files now in the playlist window, you can move them around at will. Just grab one of the titles and position it over another occupied slot. You'll see your selected file take the existing slot and push the previous file down. For now, I'll keep my files in alphabetical order, as shown in Figure 6-14.

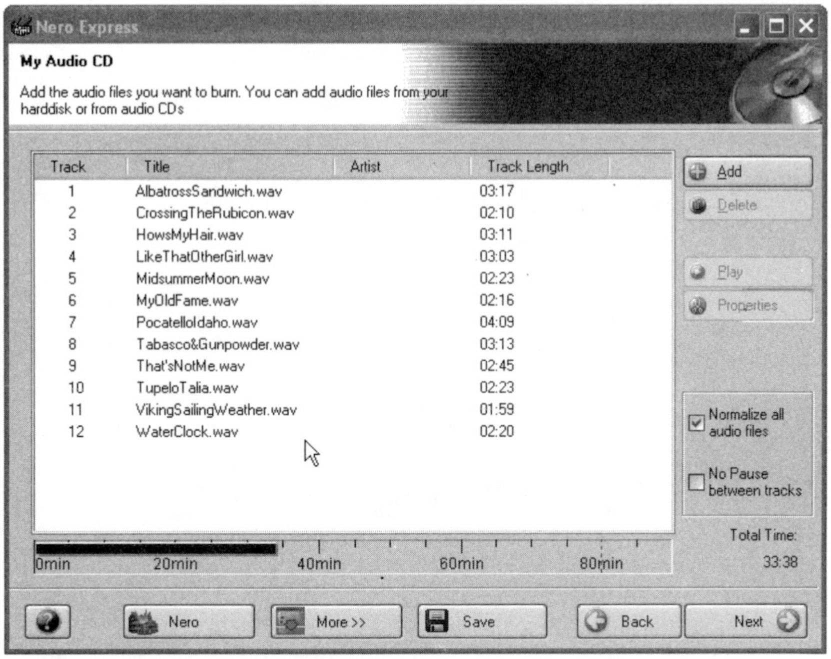

Figure 6-14
The songs are assembled in the playlist. Here, they're in alphabetical order, but it's easy to move them around.

Listen to the tunes in the playlist window to make sure they're all where you want them—location-wise and volume-wise. When you click the Next button, you'll see the final screen before you click the Burn button. Go ahead and enter the title and artist information in the appropriate text fields, as shown in Figure 6-15.

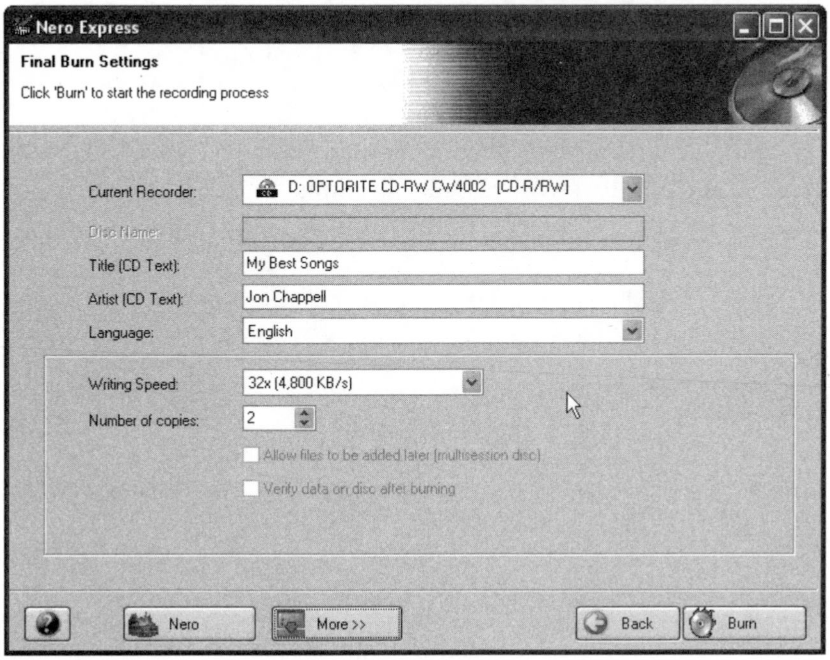

Figure 6-15
The last step before clicking the Burn button is entering optional text in the Title and Artist fields.

Load a blank CD-R (not a CD-RW) disc in the CD-RW drive and then click the More button at the bottom of the screen. This pops up the Extended Settings window, which tells you the Write Method is Disc-At-Once mode (Nero's default), as shown in Figure 6-16. Disc-At-Once mode is for burning an entire CD in a single session. You won't have to check this every time. Unless you use Track-At-Once mode (which is rare in mastering audio CDs), you'll never have to change this option.

Figure 6-16
The Extended Settings pop-up window. Keep the setting for Disc-At-Once mode.

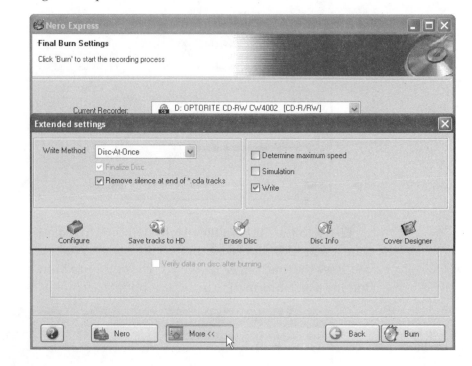

May we have a drum roll, please? Click Burn. You'll see a screen showing the activity of your blank CD being burned with your music, as shown in Figure 6-17. All you have to do now is wait.

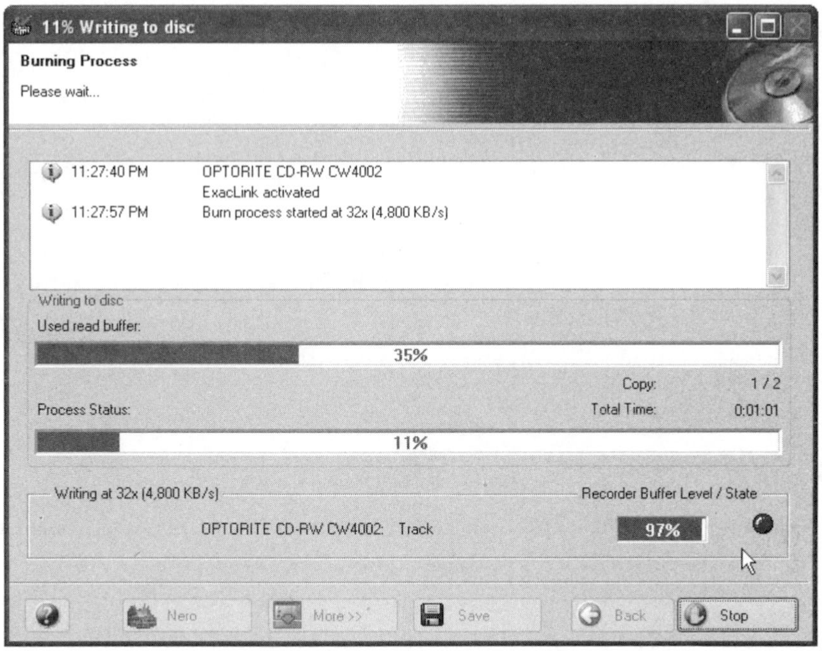

Figure 6-17
When you click Burn, Nero begins to write to your CD and apprises you of the read/write status in the process.

When the CD is finished, it will automatically eject. A quick test to perform on your newly minted CD is to walk it over to any old CD player (a boom box or DiscMan will do) and pop it in. Check to see that the total number of tracks shows up in the display. Then play a few seconds of the beginning of each track. On the last track, fast-forward to the song's remaining few seconds and listen to the very end of the CD. If all checks out, chances are you've got yourself a perfect CD. Give it a critical listen all the way through as soon as you have the time.

Creating a Data CD

Nero has you follow roughly the same procedure for creating a data CD that you do for an audio CD, whether you're writing MP3 files or making backups of your hard disk contents. Creating data CDs is also important for backup and archiving purposes, even if the process isn't quite as magical as creating a music CD. You can explore the program's options for creating hybrid CDs as well—CDs that mix data and music.

Packaging Your CD

You may have been so excited when the CD-RW drive spit out your finished CD that you didn't notice there was one more screen in the wizard's bag of tricks: the intuitively titled "What do you want to do now?" screen. Listed is a set of useful options, but the one we'll focus on now is the Cover Designer feature.

Here, you can create colorful labels for the CD itself as well as the various components of the jewel box. The process of attaching a label to the disc and inserting attractive covers in your CD's case is called *packaging*, and it's the final touch of professionalism your tracks need before they leave your care and go out into the world.

15 MINUTES

Step 9: Create Labels

In Nero Express, select Cover Designer, whose icon appears along the bottom (click More if you don't see a list of five icons). You'll be presented with an Explorer-type window, as shown in Figure 6-18. Select one of the preexisting documents, such as Rock.nct. A preview of the CD elements shows up on the right.

Figure 6-18
The New Document window in Nero Express's Cover Designer Wizard. For my CD, I've selected Rock.nct.

If you've been a diligent record keeper, you're treated to a nice surprise: The Cover Designer has taken your previously entered info and put it in the appropriate places on the CD insert card, front and back covers, and on the disc label itself. How thoughtful!

Click any one of the four tabs along the bottom to get a close-up view of the booklet front, booklet rear, inlay (the paper that goes in the back of the CD case and includes the two spines), and the disk label itself. Figure 6-19 shows a close-up of the disk label.

Figure 6-19
Clicking the Disk 1 tab shows a close-up of how the disk label will appear when it prints.

You can print on plain paper from your inkjet or laser printer, but a better way is to purchase special third-party label templates from an office-supply store. These templates, from companies such as Avery, come premade for CDs and include the proper *scoring* (serrations that make for easier and more accurate folding) for the CD inlays. You can then choose which template you'll be using from the upper-right pull-down menu, as shown in Figure 6-20. In this case, I'm using Avery 8931/5931 CD/DVD labels.

Figure 6-20
Choose from a list of
third-party templates
to print your labels
and inserts.

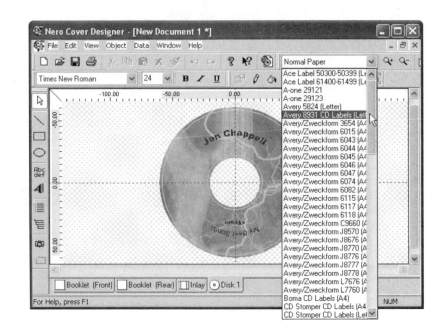

After you've made your selection, choose Print. You'll be presented with the
Print dialog box. You'll leave everything as it is in the General tab. In the Elements tab, uncheck everything you don't want printed and then select how
many copies you'd like, as shown in Figure 6-21. In this case, I'm printing two
copies of the disc label (which will print on one single sheet), so I'll uncheck the
top three boxes and change the Copies field to 2.

Figure 6-21
The Elements tab in
the Print window
allows you to select
which type of
documents you'll
print and how many.

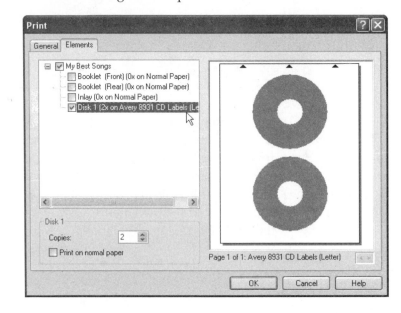

Before you select OK, make sure your printer is loaded with the proper label stock at the right orientation. On my Epson C80, I put the disc label sheet face up, top in, as shown in Figure 6-22.

Figure 6-22
Loading the Avery CD/DVD label sheet into the Epson C80 inkjet printer—head in, face up.

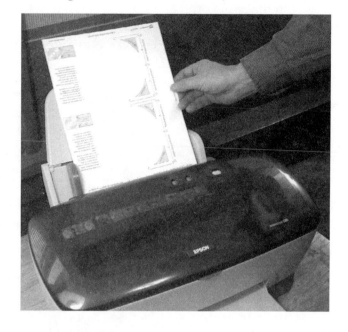

A few seconds later, my perfectly centered CD labels roll out of the printer, as shown in Figure 6-23.

Figure 6-23
The Avery template rolls out of the printer with the image perfectly centered on the adhesive disc labels.

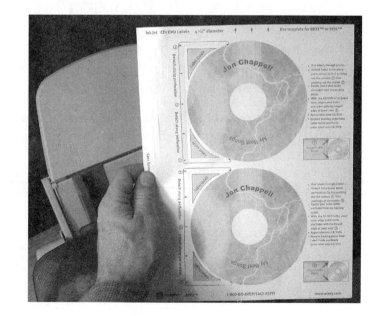

Go back and print the other types of labels, loading in the correct card stock before you click the OK button to print. Don't feel bad if you waste a couple sheets figuring out the program's quirks. The labels are cheap.

In the end, you'll end up with a CD that looks uniform and professional, as shown in Figure 6-24. What's more, you didn't hire a designer, nor did you spend hours with a magic marker and scissors creating the covers and label yourself!

Figure 6-24
The complete package: jewel box covers and CD label

Step 10: Provide Printed Matter

It's not strictly in the realm of CD production, but I'd like to throw in my two cents about what should go in the envelope along with a well-packaged CD. Following are three items in the "printed matter" department that no CD should leave home without:

❏ **Cover letter**   Write a personalized cover to whomever the package is directed—record company exec, club owner, radio jock, mother of the bride, and so on. You can offer helpful hints as to what they might find interesting within the 12 or 15 songs you're including, in case they don't have time to listen to your entire CD, or to listen to it carefully.

❏ **Lyric sheet**   If you write songs, include the lyrics so people have something to hold on to while they listen. Reading the lyrics along with the music helps them better remember the songs.

❏ **Info and bio** Don't forget to include your contact information, a brief bio of yourself or your band, and details about how your songs came into being. This should be a generic document that will serve all occasions. Think of a busy entertainment editor at a magazine who doesn't have the time to listen to your CD and form his own opinion, but must write something catchy for the weekend guide. Don't be shy about your talents! Better yet, have someone else (preferably someone who worships you) write the piece.

Putting Your Music on the Web

After you've completed the mastering stage, discussed earlier in the chapter, you don't need to burn your music to CD at all to have it heard by millions. Instead, you can upload it to the Web. Like CDs and cassette tapes, the Web must be considered as a commercially available playback and distribution medium. So for all your hard work in crafting your music and the sound of the files in the digital domain, take just a moment now to learn the relatively simple steps for putting your music on the Web.

Streaming vs. Downloading

The first question to ask yourself is whether you want your file to stream to listeners or to download in its entirety. This decision will affect what file format you convert to: RealAudio and QuickTime for streaming; WAV, WMA, AIF, and QuickTime for downloading. For most musicians, the downloading option is the way to go. True, it's not as immediate as streaming. But with broadband access to the Internet becoming more commonplace, the increased download time is not the issue it once was.

5-30 MINUTES

Step 11: Upload to a Web Site

Uploading a nonstreaming (WAV, AIF, QuickTime, MP3, WMA) music file to a Web site is no different from uploading any other file, such as a JPG or GIF file. You use an FTP (File Transfer Protocol) program to transfer the file to a directory on a Web server. Then you have to design your HTML Web page to link to it, as shown in Figure 6-25.

Figure 6-25
A Web page showing text, a photo, and a link to the MP3, which I uploaded separately using an FTP program

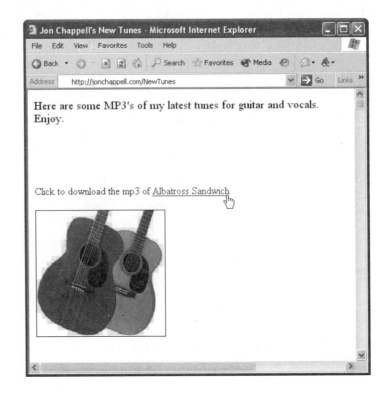

If this is all foreign to you, don't worry: Your job is just to prepare the music file. Get a Web geek friend (who probably refers to you as his "music geek" friend) to handle the logistics. Many online services, such as GeoCities and AOL, will give you disk space on which to host your own Web site, and you can easily load up an album's worth of songs for all to access.

Setting up the streaming process is a little more involved in that the server has to be specially configured to stream audio. A detailed explanation of streaming setup can be found on RealNetworks' Web site at http://realnetworks.com/resources.

2 MINUTES

Step 12: Test the Download Process

After you upload your file to the proper directory and you have a Web page with a link that points to the file, you just need to test the download. The best way to do this is use a Web browser, such as Internet Explorer, and navigate to the site as any other user would. Click the link, and the download should begin immediately, launching your chosen MP3 (or other file format) player, which then starts playing the music (see Figure 6-26).

Figure 6-26
Clicking the link
to the MP3 file
downloads the file
and launches my
default MP3 player
(in this case, Windows
Media Player).

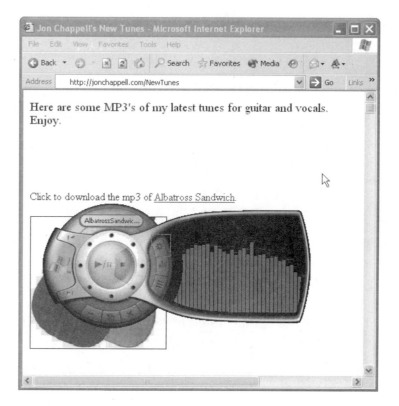

Because I hear music from my speakers, it's an indication I've done everything correctly. And if I can hear it, so can anyone else who has a Web browser
and an Internet connection. Now all I have to do is let the world know where they
can find my music. But that's a subject for another book—at least!

Moving On

It's nothing short of amazing to start with a computer and some software and end
up with a CD or MP3 that others can listen to. But the process has to be comfortable
for you, or you won't feel like doing it over and over. So one of the best things you
can do for your musical health and sanity is to create a space that's conducive to
recording. In Chapter 7 we'll explore several ways to get your home-studio environment up to speed with your recording hardware and software.

At this point you should have completed the following items:

❑ Your master mixdowns have been successfully imported into Cubase.

❑ You have applied various processes to your mixdowns to smooth out the levels and apply any last-minute tonal-balance changes.

❑ Your files can successfully be exported to MP3, WMA, and RealAudio file formats, and you understand the process for posting these files to the Web.

❑ You have burned a CD by opening Nero Express and importing the mixdown files you created in Cubase SX.

❑ You have checked your burned CD on an external audio CD player.

❑ The information you entered in Nero Express's CD-burning application shows up in the Cover Designer.

❑ You have printed labels for your CD.

Part III

Healthy and
Happy Recording

Chapter 7
Home Studio Considerations

Tools of the Trade

Speaker stands (risers) or shelving materials for placing speakers

Office furniture, including computer desk, desk chair with casters, and chair mat

Lighting dimmer kit (rheostat)

1"×8" board (18" to 20" long) or stiff mat material of same dimensions

Neoprene rubber matting (or several mouse pads)

Gloves, goggles, and a facemask (for working with fiberglass)

R-11 batt insulation

Acoustical board

Fabric (burlap or nylon)

Cordless screwdriver/drill

Circular saw/table saw (or have the lumber yard make the cuts for you)

Drywall anchors

Lumber (2×4 boards and 3/4" plywood)

Hardware (2½" wood screws, washers, and eye screws)

Caulking

Measuring tape

Staple gun

So you've got your computer up and running, and your peripherals are all passing audio in and out with abandon. It's a real accomplishment to get all the cylinders firing, but in music creation, just as in driving a car, a satisfying experience isn't limited to a smooth-running engine.

Other environmental elements need to be in place if you're to endure, let alone enjoy, hours upon hours of recording music. So once you get your sound-generating gear operational, it's time to turn your attention to your surroundings.

In this chapter we'll consider all the factors in the music-making process, *except* for the computer. As much work as it may be to set up your computer to record music, it's just as important to create an environment around that machine conducive to music-making, because that's what you'll appreciate day in, day out, long after you take your computer's ability to crunch numbers for granted.

A Sense of Space

The computer will perform the same regardless of whether you stuff it in a dark closet or seat it in a formal dining room. But humans are a little more finicky. The environment you create for your music-making efforts has to be comfortable, creatively inspiring, and *fun* to be in. Not only for you, but for anyone with you.

As a first step, try to choose a space that will suit you *personally*, regardless of the activity you plan to engage in. That might mean choosing the lesser of several evils. Ask yourself, Do I want to set up in the corner of the bedroom where there's less room, or in the basement where there's less heat? Do I want to be in the garage where there's no carpet, or in the family room where's there's less privacy? After choosing whichever room is best, you can then take steps to improve its atmosphere for music production. Let's first examine how the pros do it to see what we can learn from their example.

Two Rooms vs. One Room

In a professional or commercial recording studio, at least two rooms are devoted to the recording process. The *control room* holds all the equipment, such as the mixer, the computer, the outboard effects, and the monitor speakers. The control room is also where the engineer, producer, and other non-musicians (such as the client or record-company executive) hang out (see Figure 7-1).

Figure 7-1
Pro studios separate
the recording process
into two spaces:
the control room
and the studio.

Courtesy of Catasonic Studios; Alec Boehm, photographer

The *studio*, or *live room*, holds the musicians and has very little equipment in it other than microphones and whatever gear the musicians need to create their music. The studio is typically adjacent to the control room, separated by a wall with a large, multipaned window to allow visual communication between the musicians and the control room personnel (see Figure 7-2). Verbal communication is accomplished electronically through the microphones in the studio (so that the musicians can speak to the control room) and through the musicians' headphones (which allows the control room, via a "talkback" mic, to speak to the band).

Figure 7-2
The control room and
studio are separated
by thick glass panes,
which allow visual
communication but
prevent sound from
creeping through.

Courtesy of Catasonic Studios; Alec Boehm, photographer

To play along with previously recorded tracks, the musicians wear headphones, which allow them to hear the tracks but prevent the sound from going through the mics that are set up to record just the instruments. The people in the control room listen over speakers, which provide a more realistic picture of the final product. Because they're isolated from the studio, the control room personnel hear the live instruments (cranking away on the other side of the glass) only over the speakers and in balance with the prerecorded tracks.

Because there are no microphones in the control room (except for the talkback mic), the engineer, producer, and others are free to speak whenever they like—during the recording process, between takes, and so on. The vibe in the studio is very different: The musicians don't talk much at all, except between takes, and then usually only with minimal discussion and a quiet intensity. Musicians play, stop, and wait for the reaction in the control room to come through the talkback mic.

When you record and perform in the same space, as most of us at home do, it helps to understand the different mind sets of a control room facilitator versus a studio performer. Often as not, you'll be serving in both functions, switching back and forth with dizzying frequency.

Because most people don't have the luxury of devoting two rooms to the recording process, we'll focus on optimizing one room for both studio and control room activities.

Placing Equipment

Because the computer is the center of your musical operation, you might be tempted to place it front and center—say, within arm's reach of your right hand. But because a computer is noisy (due primarily to its cooling fans) and bulky, it's better to place it off of the desktop and out of the way. Keep just the monitor in a central location.

You will, of course, need access to the CPU periodically—when installing software or plugging in cables—but the most physical interaction many of us have with the computer box itself is pressing the power switch. After that, most of our activity is conducted via the mouse or the keyboard.

A good solution is to keep the computer on the floor under your desk. This not only keeps the desktop free and clear but allows the desktop surface itself to act as a sound barrier that somewhat inhibits the fan noise from hitting your ears directly.

If you have a thick carpet under the desk, place the computer on a thin, hard surface (such as a 1"×8" plank of wood) so that its feet keep the case from coming into direct contact with the carpet (see Figure 7-3). And just because you place it under a desk doesn't mean that it should be stuffed into a corner, because this might promote heat buildup—a bad thing for computers. Also, keep in mind you will need access to its CD or DVD drives, and less frequently its rear-panel ports and connections. If your equipment is going inside existing furniture or against cabinetry, be sure to allow for holes (service loops) so that you can feed the cables through.

Figure 7-3
A computer placed under a desk, on a plank of wood. Note that the plank keeps the computer case from touching the floor and aids in air flow.

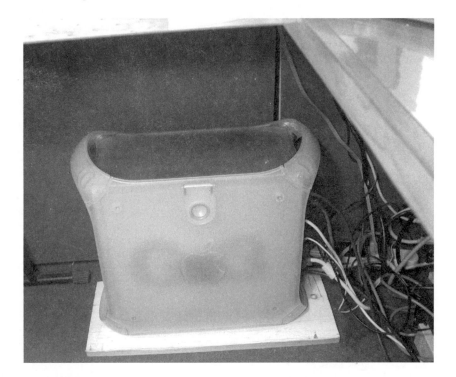

Monitor Placement

Although you can put your computer almost anywhere that's convenient, the placement of your monitor speakers is much more critical. The ideal position for studio monitors is in an equilateral triangle with your head (see Figure 7-4), when you assume your normal listening position for mixing. This means the distance between the speakers is the same as the distance from your head to either speaker. For most nearfield monitors, a distance of three to five feet is ideal.

Figure 7-4
An aerial view of the equilateral triangle formed by the correct placing of monitors

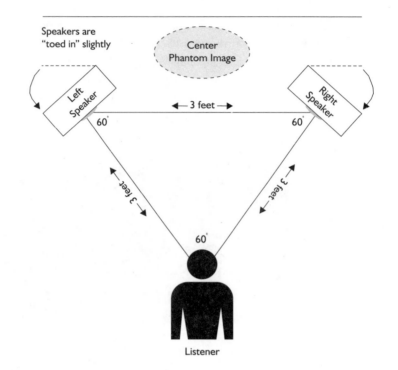

You have three practical options for positioning the monitors in your home studio:

- ❑ On speaker stands that sit on the floor and raise the speakers four to five feet above the floor (at the same height as your head)
- ❑ On shelves mounted to the back wall
- ❑ On the desktop itself, raised to the appropriate height

Using speaker stands is the best solution, assuming you have room behind your desk, but this is also the most expensive. Shelves are fairly easy to construct, even for the most reluctant carpenter. Just be sure to use padding between the speaker bottoms and the shelf to prevent unwanted vibrations and rattling.

If you elect to put your speakers on the desk, you should isolate them from the desktop's surface to prevent the speakers from vibrating. Placing them first on a some sort of riser and then sticking a couple of neoprene rubber pads between the bottom of the speakers and the riser will help keep unwanted vibrations from influencing the sound, and prevent the speakers from walking.

Once you have your speakers in position and have staked out your listening position, it's time to place the rest of your gear around that area.

TIPS OF THE TRADE

Speaker of the Mouse

A couple of neoprene mouse pads work well for stopping speakers from vibrating. Speakers have been known to "walk" right off a hard desktop if left unattended!

Sample Setups

Moving your gear around into the optimal working setup is kind of like a three-dimensional jigsaw puzzle: You know there's probably one right way to organize your specific gear, but it's pretty hard to know what that is until you try placing the pieces together through trial and error. Sometimes measuring the units and experimenting with scale drawings (with graph paper or a computer drawing program) will help, but that really only helps to avoid the situations that clearly won't work.

Your particular setup will depend on the dimensions of your individual gear and the space you have available, but generally there are three approaches (in order of ascending desirability): the tier, the L, and the U. The L shape is popular because it needs less room than the U shape and is roomier than the tiered approach. The U shape is more "cockpit like" and puts gear within easier reach, but it requires you to have three sides devoted to your music gear, something the standard home office or bedroom doesn't easily accommodate.

The Tier

Figures 7-5 shows a tiered approach, where all the gear is set up along one wall. The piano keyboard can be put on a slide-out drawer or on a keyboard stand whose height can be adjusted precisely so that the top of the keyboard slips under the tabletop. Some people like to put their computer keyboard on a sliding drawer because this puts the keyboard lower than the tabletop—a more comfortable position for marathon typing. But it's not that necessary for music production, because you won't be doing that much sustained typing on the computer keyboard.

Figure 7-5
The tiered approach lets you put all your equipment on one wall, stacking items on shelves or sliding them under the desktop.

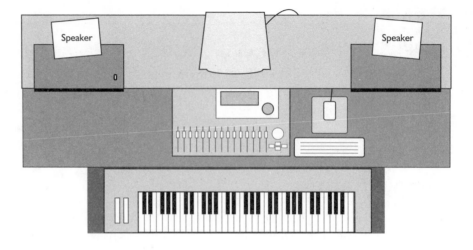

The L

The L puts the piano keyboard on the side of the desktop, which is handy for overdubbing and other situations when you need constant access to your controller (see Figure 7-6). It's a little more convenient to have the keyboard always out and ready rather than having to slide it in and out from underneath your desktop.

Figure 7-6
An L setup allows you to keep your piano keyboard in a permanent state of readiness, and it's more comfortable than the tiered approach for simultaneously accessing the computer keyboard and piano keyboard.

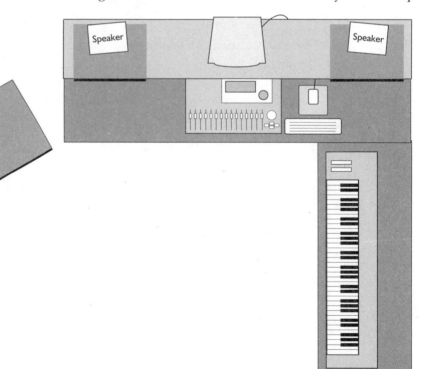

TIPS OF THE TRADE

Roscoe vs. Louie

I prefer to put my piano keyboard on the right because I'm right-handed and can perform more dexterous moves—whether that's a flute flourish, a funky bass line, or a compound pitch-bend move on a controller. If I need to run the transport functions (record, stop, play, and rewind), I use the alphanumeric keyboard with my left hand.

The U

The U shape requires the most room because it has desktop surfaces on three sides, but it's a great way to make music. The primary advantage of the U is that it leaves a dedicated mixing region in the center of the area, the crossbar of the U (see Figure 7-7). This is one of the hallmarks of a pro studio because critical listening tasks are performed here—and the more pristine that space is, the better.

Figure 7-7
The U shape lets you dedicate a region just for mixing and monitoring—the most critical and exacting tasks in music production after performing.

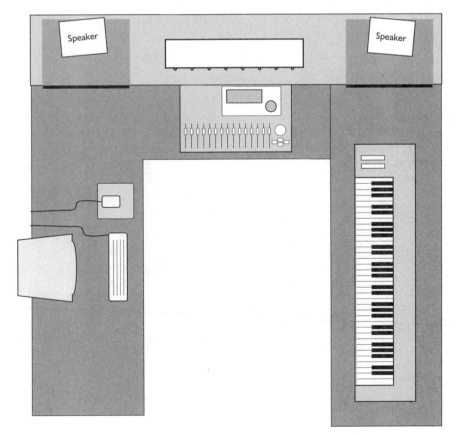

Ergonomics 101

Having a comfortable work environment is not only conducive to creativity, it's essential for your health and well-being when spending long hours on music. Comfort is largely a personal issue, based on your body type, age, and tastes, but a few standard practices have proven themselves to be particularly useful to music-makers.

Give 'Em the Chair

An easy chair or couch may be the most comfortable piece of seating furniture for watching TV or playing video games, but for computers and music you want a good desk chair with casters (see Figure 7-8). The casters are important because you'll spend lots of time rolling around to access various components in your setup: computer keyboard, piano keyboard, mixer, guitar, and so on.

In professional recording studios, the floors of the control room are usually hardwood—parquet being a popular choice. In a home studio or office, or indeed any room in a residence, the floors tend to have carpets or rugs covering them. Consider getting one of those hard plastic sheets that go under the chairs. This will let you scoot around your studio without sacrificing the carpeted motif of the room.

Figure 7-8
Invest in a good desk chair with casters. The "scoot" factor increases if you put a hard mat underfoot (wheel).

TIPS OF THE TRADE

Desk Chair de Milo

Guitarists should consider a desk chair with detachable arms, or even a model with no arms at all. It's very difficult to play guitar in a chair with arms—and even harder to pick it up and put it down quickly.

Of Tabletops and Drawers

You don't need any custom furniture for music creation, but it's nice to have computer furniture for a setup involving any kind of computer work, because accommodations usually include desk space for your monitor, a slide-out drawer for the keyboard, and in some cases a special cradle or rack for the CPU—good for keeping the computer out of the way of the desktop and your ears (see Figure 7-9).

Figure 7-9
Computer furniture is a good start for music creation because it puts the keyboard a little lower than the height of a standard tabletop, has a space for the monitor, and usually allows you to put the computer out of the way of your desktop space.

Photo courtesy of Anthro Corp at www.anthro.com

Let There Be Lighting

Creating music doesn't require any special room lighting unless you plan to do a lot of music reading. Then the same rules apply that would for reading a book: Get a good desk lamp and aim it at the reading material.

But most people don't read that much music when recording, at least with the intensity and length that you would when learning a piano sonata. Reading a computer screen doesn't require any light, of course, because the monitor radiates its own light from within the case.

Dim the Glims

One nice touch you can add in the lighting department of your recording studio is a dimmer (also called a *rheostat*). Sometimes having an overhead light blazing away at 100 or 150 watts all the time just doesn't inspire the right vibe—especially when you're doing a blues ballad, late at night, after a long day at the office. Wouldn't it be nice to knock those incandescents down a lumen or two?

With a dimmer, you can. Dimmers are best used for existing wall switches that control overhead lights (see Figure 7-10). You can buy them at any hardware store, and they don't require any special skill to install, *assuming you know how to turn off the power to that switch.* You must be extremely careful because you're dealing with high voltage. Be sure to turn off the circuit breaker that controls the switch before you install the dimmer. If you can't do this for any reason, have an electrician do it for you.

Figure 7-10
Putting in a dimmer allows you to soften the overhead lighting of your studio, enhancing the atmosphere.

HEADS UP!

Proceed with Extreme Caution
Replacing a light switch may be a fairly simple operation, but it can be extremely dangerous because you're dealing with high-voltage electricity. Unless you are completely comfortable shutting off the main power in your service box or throwing the right circuit breaker, do not attempt this operation yourself.

Another solution to affect atmospheric lighting is to position three-way lamps strategically around the room. Then you can just turn the overheads off. That way, you can turn on some or all the lamps selectively and at various brightness levels. Ambience is often overlooked in recording, but remember that even though you're *recording*, music *creation* is just as much about the process as the end result.

HEADS UP!

Electricity and Noise

Bear in mind that any electrical alteration has the potential to affect the ambient noise of the room. Low-cost dimmers, and especially the dreaded fluorescent lighting fixture, can create a constant and fatal hum in your audio system, depending on the quality of the wiring in your studio space. Always test new electrical fixtures with your audio system on immediately after installing and before finishing the area around the new electrical work, or installing any final trim to the fixture itself, so you can easily remove the new component if it is a noise source.

Practicing Sound Reasoning in Acoustics

Professional recording studios spend thousands of dollars to treat their rooms for soundproofing and acoustics. Home recordists who are serious about creating a neutral environment, and who have earmarked funds for this, might construct a floating room, insulate the four walls with special material, and purchase movable baffles. But more likely than not, you'll spend your money on more tangible items, such as a spare hard drive or a software-based sampler.

For our hypothetical room, we'll consider several approaches to taming sound, none of which costs very much money or requires that much effort or expertise. Even hanging a winter coat in the corner or facing an acoustic guitar toward an overstuffed couch instead of the wall can help you either reduce reflected sound or isolate an instrument when recording.

For the computer recordist, the philosophy of room sound is sort of a black-and-white proposition: If you can't make the room an acoustic paradise, then you want to deaden it almost completely and add any ambient treatment (such as reverb) after the fact (i.e., during mixdown), electronically. Because you'll be recording (which can require isolation) and mixing (which should be done in a neutral room), the best compromise is to go for a deadened sound.

Leakage and Isolation for the Sonic Fuel Spill

Recordists give careful consideration to the twin issues of isolation and leakage. Why not just throw up a mic and be done with it, you ask? Well, in many cases you can. And that's how most live recording is done. But if you want control over the balance and sound of each element, you have to record instruments on separate tracks with little or no leakage from other instruments.

Leakage is only an issue with acoustic recording, or recording with an open mic, and only when other sound sources are present (speakers, other instruments, or noise). It's also only a problem when you're multitracking or when you want each instrument going to its own track so that you can balance and process them later (during the mixdown stage).

If you mic up two musicians playing together in the same room without isolating them, then each mic picks up a little of the other source. For example, suppose you have a drummer and a guitar player recording simultaneously in the same room. When both musicians are playing, it's not a problem, because each instrument "masks" the presence of the other in its own mic. But if you want to drop one instrument out in the mixdown (such as the drums) to hear just the guitar playing solo, you'll still hear the drums coming through the guitar track, even though you turned down completely the drum track.

Conversely, if you decide to replace the guitar part, either by punching in or overdubbing on a separate track and erasing the original, you'd still be stuck with the old guitar part heard faintly as part of the drum track—and that could be disastrous to the groove.

Leakage, or *bleed,* can also become a problem in signal processing. Adding a low-frequency boost to the guitar will also cause the bass drum bleed to become more prominent—even though you haven't touched the drum track at all. Similarly, if you boost the highs on the guitar part—say, to bring out the "sproingy" sound of the strings in a scratchy funk-rhythm part—the cymbals would now start to sound crisper and more brittle.

When you have bleed on a track, you can't make adjustments to one sound without also affecting the other. Sometimes this is okay, but many times it's not, and you're stuck with no way to eradicate the "ghost" instrument that haunts your track and refuses to leave.

It's important to clear up one key issue in matters of room sound: Sound-proofing is an entirely different issue from sound treatment. Soundproofing deals with keeping outside sound out and the inside sound in. As simple as that sounds, it can be very difficult and expensive to achieve.

Sound treatment limits itself to only what happens to the sound inside the room and is much more manageable to recordists on a budget. Here, you don't concern yourself with outside sound getting in (such as a nearby train whistle or truck traffic) or inside sound escaping (and bothering housemates and neighbors). There are easy ways around this, such as scheduling and forgiveness. To truly soundproof a room, however, involves construction, cinderblocks, air traps, insulation, floating rooms, decoupling, and other scary-sounding and scientific principles.

This doesn't mean that sound treatment, when done correctly and effectively, is cheap. However, you can achieve varying degrees of success using just sweat equity (which used to be called "elbow grease") and some inexpensive, readily available materials.

Treat That Sound

Because actual soundproofing is beyond the scope of this book (and because it doesn't actually affect the sound quality of a recording), we'll focus solely on sound *treatment*. Most of our efforts will be devoted to reducing reflections from the walls and other surfaces in the room. This involves the processes of absorption and diffusion—also known as *deadening*. This is not so much stomping the life out of a sound as it is neutralizing the room's influence, which can limit the ambient treatment you supply later on in the process (such as during mixdown).

Materialism

A professional studio is built with no parallel surfaces (wall to wall, floor to ceiling) because these pose problematic reflections (called *standing waves)* that interfere with recording and listening back (monitoring). Because most other rooms in the world *do* have parallel walls, you have to treat those surfaces to prevent them from reflecting sound in a bad way.

The best way to squelch reflections from the walls' hard surfaces is to place absorbent materials on them. Because hanging shag carpeting from the wall looks tacky, you might consider using acoustic foam from a company such as Auralex (www.auralex.com) that makes scientifically designed acoustic-treatment materials (see Figure 7-11).

Figure 7-11
Auralex makes a
variety of materials
for all sorts of
acoustical
applications,
including absorption
and diffusion of
sound reflections.

Alternatively, you could construct absorptive panels yourself that you can hang like a big picture (the bigger the better). When you're done recording, just remove them and stash them in a closet or behind a couch.

A Panel Discussion

To build a panel, create a 2'×4' frame out of 2×4's and cover one side with plywood. Then fill the frame with insulation, such as regular household R-11 fiberglass batts. Finally, enclose the open side of the frame with a one-inch-thick acoustical board or panel, such as those made by Owens Corning (series 700) or Knauf (Black Acoustical Board). Your panel should look something like Figure 7-12.

Proper Attire for Working with Fiberglass
While working with fiberglass, you must wear goggles, gloves, a mask, and a long-sleeved shirt.

Figure 7-12
An acoustical
panel is easy to build
with some wood,
insulation, screws and
washers, and acoustic
paneling. Oh, and
don't forget the
cordless screwdriver!

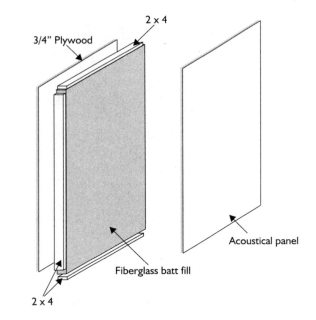

3/4" Plywood

2 x 4

Acoustical panel

Fiberglass batt fill

2 x 4

HEADS UP!

Double-check Your Toolbox

You should be able to construct four panels in an afternoon (two to three hours). Buy your lumber and hardware in one trip, and make sure you have all the tools you need before you leave for the hardware store or lumber yard.

How you hang the panels is up to you, but whether you use drywall anchors or drive nails into wall studs, be sure to make careful measurements as to where each panel will go. And as always, remember the carpenter's rule: Measure twice, cut once!

Where will you put these well-crafted panels? The best place for one or two panels is the back wall opposite the speakers, behind your head. Additional panels can be placed on the side walls, directly facing your ears (see Figure 7-13).

Figure 7-13
Place absorptive panels behind you so that sound coming from the monitor speakers won't bounce back as reflected sound that interferes with the speakers' direct sound.

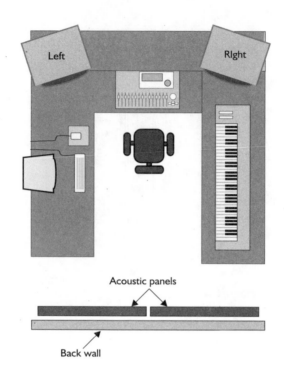

Strategically placing absorptive panels like this will help you hear only the direct sound of the speakers, and not the reflected sound, which, when mixed with the direct sound, yields an unrealistic version of what has actually been recorded.

Parts list for constructing four 2'x4' acoustic panels

	Material	Size	Qty.
Frame	2x4	3'9"	8
	2x4	2'	8
Back Panel	3/4" Plywood	2'x4'	4 (one 4'x8' sheet cut into four 2'x4' sections)
Front Panel	1" Acoustical panel	2'x4'	4
Covering	Burlap or nylon	3'x5' (enough to stretch around 2'x4' front panel and behind frame)	4
Hardware	Staples (to tack covering to frame)	large (staple gun size)	1 box (~32/panel)
	Wood screws (to build frame and attach panels)	2-1/2"	1 box (~16/panel)
	Washers (to prevent screw heads from punching through acoustical panel)	3/4" diameter	32 (8/panel)

Baffles

A *baffle* is a partition that prevents sound waves from passing through it, used to keep two regions acoustically isolated from each other. Baffles don't work 100 percent, but used correctly, they cut down on enough leakage or bleed into microphones to make them very useful in everyday recording situations. Several different types of baffles are used in recording. Let's look at the four most popular.

Gobos

The name *gobo* is applied to a portable, floor-standing baffle that can be moved around to selectively isolate an instrument from bleeding into another area or mic. Whereas wall and ceiling baffles are used for mixing, gobos are used for recording. You often find guitar amps heavily guarded by gobos because their loud volume and speaker-generated sound tend to permeate every part of the studio, if not kept in check.

You can turn an acoustical panel into a gobo by creating two "feet" for it, as pictured in Figure 7-14. Be sure to make the gap between vertical pieces just the right width so that the panel fits snugly inside the support.

Figure 7-14
With just a few pieces of wood and a saw that can cut a 45-degree angle (or a miter box if you're using a hand saw), you can make feet for your acoustic panel, turning it into a portable sound shield.

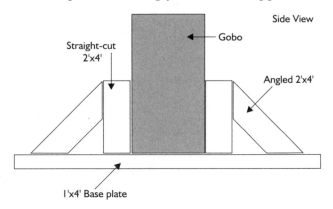

Ceiling Baffles

The ceiling is a hard surface, just like a wall, and can often contribute unwanted reflections. Especially if the ceiling is low, a hanging baffle is useful in mixing because it prevents the monitors' direct sound from mixing with the ceiling-reflected sound.

There's no difference in the construction of a baffle meant for the wall versus one for the ceiling, just in the method in attaching it (see Figure 7-15). Alternatively, you could construct a special lightweight frame for a single piece of acoustic board to be your ceiling baffle, using 1'×2' framing instead of the much heavier 2'×4's.

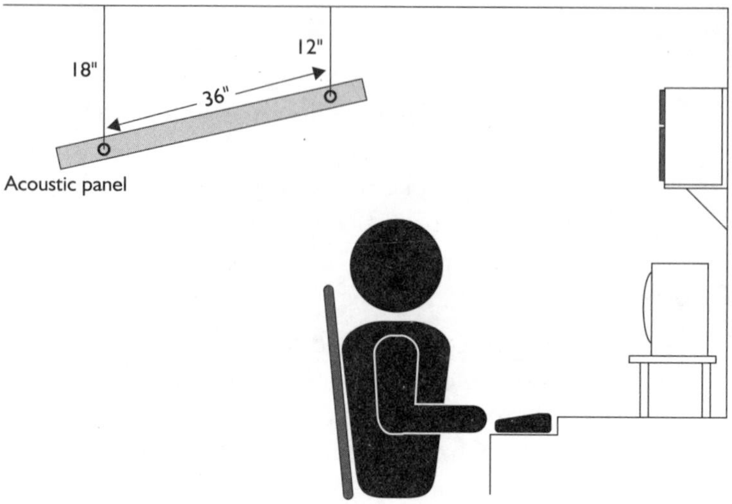

Figure 7-15
A ceiling baffle helps prevent unwanted reflections emanating from the ceiling. Sloping the baffle, so that the rear hangs below the front, is a common practice.

18" 12" 36"

Acoustic panel

HEADS UP!

Hanging Baffles Securely and Safely

Because the baffles we've constructed are fairly heavy, be sure to use the correctly rated drywall anchors for ceiling hanging. Picture wire or florist's wire is usually heavy duty enough to keep the hanging baffle steady. Use eye screws for a secure tie-off point for the wire.

Hanging Tough

Though drywall anchors will work on lighter material and panels, toggle bolts make for more secure attachment to drywall ceilings. A good method for hanging anything large from a ceiling involves securing the medium to large hooks in the ceiling joists, then using short lengths of chain (easily obtainable now at home-improvement stores) to hang the panel. The chains provide stronger support and make the angle at which the panel hangs easily adjustable by selecting different links on individual chains to connect to the hooks in the ceiling and on the panel.

TIPS OF THE TRADE

Light and Easy

As a super-lightweight alternative, you can just use black acoustical board, which will attach to the ceiling easily, without the need to drill in drywall anchors and screws.

Tent Baffles

If for any reason you can't access, influence, or otherwise touch the walls of your room, consider surrounding yourself with sound-absorbent material on three, four, or even fives sides (if you include the area over your head). The tent baffle can be a cozy solution when you have to mark off territory for your workspace in a much larger room.

The easiest way to construct a tent is to attach curtain rods from the ceiling and then hang drapery, curtain, or blankets from them. The heavier the material, the better—and if you can get theatrical curtains, or *blacks,* that's the best of all. But they're pretty expensive, and of course, the heavier the material, the stronger your support structure must be. Figure 7-16 shows a simple tent structure.

Rattle and Hum

If you go with conventional curtains, be sure to get cloth loops, not metal or plastic, because these can rattle during recording and mixing.

Figure 7-16
A tent baffle provides some sound isolation as well as some visual privacy.

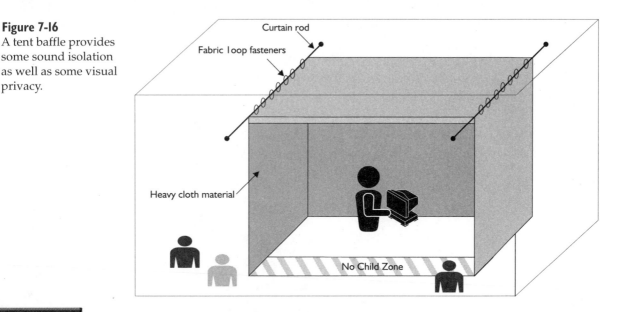

Double Your Fun

If you're really looking for isolation, you can construct a double-tent assembly. Just be sure to leave 6" of air in between the two tents, because dead space is an important factor in sound absorption between materials.

Bass Traps

Acoustic panels and tent baffles are good at preventing mid- and high-frequency reflections, but they're powerless against the oozing low-end frequencies that can creep through your studio.

Bass frequencies can literally move around corners, and to tame them you need special devices called *bass traps*. Good bass traps can cost several hundred dollars, but you can make your own for relatively little money. Although not as good as a unit designed by Auralex, Real Traps, or other companies specializing in acoustic treatment, a home-made trap is better than letting the low-end menace go unchallenged completely.

An effective bass trap can made out of a large cylinder, which is also called a *tube trap*. Constructing a tube trap is fairly easy once you secure the right materials (making it look nice is another matter!).

Build a Better Bass Trap

To make a tube trap, start with a large cylinder, three feet in length and about 20 inches in diameter. A good source for this is pipe insulation, which is sold by companies such as Knauf (www.knauf.com) in various configurations. The large diameter helps to mitigate frequencies in the 40–100 Hz range. Make caps for the two ends out of plywood or drywall and caulk them onto the ends of the tube, making an air-tight seal. Then cover the tube with the included adhesive-backed paper or add your own fabric (see Figure 7-17).

Figure 7-17
A fabric covered cylinder, if it has a fairly large diameter (10 inches or more), makes a good bass trap.

TIPS OF THE TRADE

Setting Traps

Bass traps are most effective when set up in corners, particularly where hard walls are at 90-degree angles to each other. For detailed plans on a really cool DIY bass trap, visit Jon Gale's Web site at http://ic.net/~jtgale/diy2.htm.

Cords, Cables, and Wires

The computer-based recording studio doesn't have nearly the amount of cables and cords that a conventional or older, component-based studio has. That's because so many of the processes are internal—bridged via software wires instead of between physical boxes, as the Rack Rear view of Propellerhead's Reason shows in Figure 7-18.

Figure 7-18
What used to take a whole stack of boxes—and the cabling to connect it all—can be done internally within the computer, eliminating the need for extra wires, which can introduce their own set of problems.

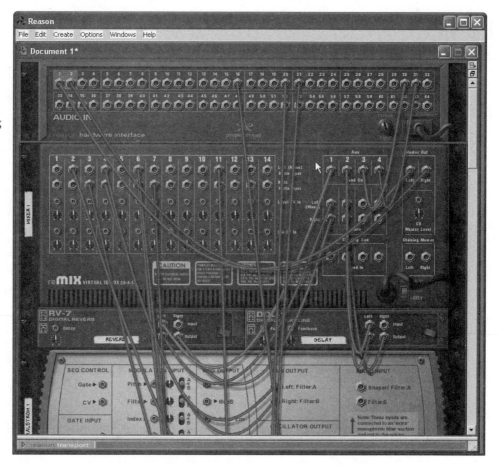

Still, the well-appointed studio, even of the computer persuasion, has a healthy amount of cables coursing through it. When hooking up your gear, you'll probably tackle the cabling needs one at a time. But sooner or later, you'll find you have a snake pit underfoot, and you'll have to deal with cables as a separate issue. So this section helps you know your electrical spaghetti.

Types of Cables

It helps to think of cables not by their length or their color but by their function. A cable transports a signal, of course, but in music and audio recording, a cable carries only one of three types of signal: audio, data, or power. (A power cord is a fairly straightforward concept, so we don't need to devote much thought to it.) The type of connector at the end of an audio or data cable further defines its function within that category. Following is a look at both the connectors and the functions of the various cables.

It All Comes Down to Three

Although there may be only three types of signals in music production—audio, data, and power—there are many different connectors for the different formats those signals can take. Learn to establish first which type of the three signals you're dealing with before considering the connector.

Audio

These transport analog audio, or "actual music" that, when put through a speaker or headphones, produce music. Audio is the most fragile of the three types of signals, and it doesn't take much to corrupt it—introducing hum or noise into the system. So buy high-quality cables from music stores, rather than a no-label brand at a consumer electronics store (though these will certainly serve their purpose in a pinch). Following are the different types of connectors you'll find on audio cables.

1/8" Stereo

Also known as "mini," this is the type of connection used for DiscMan and MP3 player headphones (see Figure 7-19). The 1/8" jack is found on soundcards for both mic inputs and speaker outputs. Apple still builds them into their Macintosh computers. You can convert a 1/8" stereo cable into other types of connections through adapters.

Figure 7-19
The 1/8″ (mini) connection is used for consumer-level headphones and is found on many soundcards.

1/4″ Mono or Stereo

Mono 1/4″ cables are unbalanced, consisting of a *tip* and a *sleeve* (and are sometimes referred to as *TS)* for signal and ground. These include *instrument cables,* which are used to connect guitars, keyboards, and drum machines, and *line-level cables,* used for hooking together components. Line-level cables can have either RCA (sometimes called *Phono)* plugs on them or 1/4″ plugs.

Stereo 1/4″ cables consist of a tip, ring, and sleeve, and they can be used to carry three kinds of signals:

- ❏ Balanced audio (tip = + signal; ring = - signal; sleeve = ground)
- ❏ Stereo (tip = left channel; ring = right channel; sleeve = ground)
- ❏ Send/return for a stereo insert jack (tip = send; ring = return; sleeve = ground)

As if this weren't versatile enough, a stereo 1/4″ plug can substitute for a mono 1/4″ plug (but not vice versa). Figure 7-20 shows mono and stereo 1/4″ plugs side by side.

Figure 7-20
A 1/4″ mono (left) and stereo plug. The stereo plug can also be used for balanced audio and send-and-return functions.

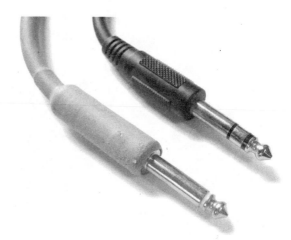

RCA

This connector features a center post and surrounding flange, which looks like a castle turret (see Figure 7-21). RCA cables carry unbalanced audio and are commonly found on home stereo gear. You can easily convert an RCA to a 1/4" TS plug or jack with an adapter. (RCA plugs and jacks are also used for S/PDIF data—see the section entitled "S/PDIF," later in this chapter.)

Figure 7-2l
An RCA (also called *Phono)* cable carries unbalanced audio and S/PDIF data, and it's found on soundcards and consumer stereo systems.

XLR

An XLR connection has a three-pronged plug that carries balanced audio (see Figure 7-22). Electrically identical to 1/4" balanced lines, XLR connections use more heavy-duty wire and insulation, and they're found in microphones, P.A. connections, and balanced-line situations where a more robust approach to cabling is warranted. (XLR is also used for AES/EBU data.)

Figure 7-22
An XLR connection and cable are ideal for balanced audio in high-end audio applications (and also used for AES/ EBU data).

Balanced vs. Unbalanced

In a balanced audio line, the signal is split into two paths at the device's output jack. The balanced plug on the cable reverses the phase (polarity) of one of the signals. As the two signals travel down the cable length, they'll pick up noise identically—AC hum, radio signals, and so on. When the signals reach the receiving end, the phase-reversed signal is reversed again (restoring it to its original phase) and combined with the original signal. This processes is called *summing*.

The two summed audio signals are now in phase, but the noise picked up in both wires is now perfectly *out of phase* and therefore cancels itself out, leaving an almost pure audio signal.

Balanced audio runs at hotter output levels than unbalanced audio. Because of this and its noise-rejecting properties, it's the format of choice for professional audio applications. But if you keep your cable lengths short—and fend off ground loops, radio interference, and other audio gremlins—you'll get just as good results with unbalanced lines as with balanced ones. Most home and semi-professional gear is designed for unbalanced use or can accept both unbalanced and balanced connections.

Data

Data signals include everything from MIDI to computer messages to digital clock. It's important to remember that MIDI, although it usually makes music in the final analysis (by driving a synth module or triggering a hard disk sample), is a data connection. Following are some of the different types of data connections you'll encounter.

MIDI

An acronym for Musical Instrument Digital Interface, MIDI uses a five-pin connection, arranged in a semicircle (see Figure 7-23). It's unidirectional, so you need two cables to establish an in and out connection between any two pieces of gear. But one MIDI cable can carry up to 16 separate channels.

Figure 7-23
MIDI is unidirectional, so it requires two cables for two-way communication. But it can carry up to 16 channels.

S/PDIF

Pronounced *ess-pee-diff* or *SPIH-diff*, S/PDIF is short for Sony/Philips Digital Interface. It's a stereo digital-audio protocol (unidirectional) that transfers a signal across an instrument cable with RCA plugs, or via Toslink (after Toshiba, who invented it) fiber-optic cables (see Figure 7-24).

Figure 7-24
S/PDIF can travel over RCA or Toslink (fiber optic) connections.

ADAT Lightpipe

Lightpipe is the name given to Alesis' eight-channel digital-audio protocol (see Figure 7-25), which travels over Toslink fiber-optic cables. Lightpipe is a standard, and many digital mixers and audio interfaces sport ADAT Lightpipe connections.

Figure 7-25
Lightpipe is Alesis'
eight-channel optical
protocol, which has
been accepted as a
standard among
audio manufacturers.

TDIF

TDIF stands for TASCAM Digital Interface. This is TASCAM's digital-audio format, which carries digital multitrack, digital audio, and sync information, and it uses a computer-style 25-pin connector, called a DB25 (see Figure 7-26).

Figure 7-26
TDIF is similar to
Alesis' Lightpipe, but
it outputs multichannel
digital audio and sync
over a computer-style
DB25 connection.

AES/EBU

AES/EBU stands for Audio Engineering Society/European Broadcast Union. This format carries stereo digital audio via an XLR connection (see Figure 7-27). It's used largely in Europe in professional-level audio applications.

Figure 7-27
AES/EBU signals
travel over standard
XLR connections.

BNC

Also called a *bayonet* connection, because of the twisting motion used to lock it into place (like affixing a bayonet to a rifle), BNC uses a center pin and sleeve to make Word Clock connections (see Figure 7-28).

Figure 7-28
BNC is used for Word Clock connections.

Cable Quality

Like everything else in this world, cables can be good or bad. Good cables, not surprisingly, cost more than bad cables, and they have more robust plugs and better shielding and insulation. A good tip-off that a cable is of high quality is that it has metal connectors; cheap cables have molded plastic ends (see Figure 7-29).

Figure 7-29
High-quality cables, such as those made by Galaxy Audio, are your best insurance against unwanted dropouts, pops, and buzzes.

Cable Tips

Plugging and unplugging cables is something you'll do a lot in your studio. Quickly determining what type of cable you need to connect up your gear or to perform a certain function saves time. Plus, it makes you look like you know what you're doing in front of your friends. Here are some tips that will help you organize and utilize your cable collection:

❏ Have extras of every type of cable, in various lengths, so that you can add pieces to your existing setup and so that you can move pieces around quickly and without too little or too much cable length.

❏ Run AC cords away from audio cables. The current in a power cord has an electrical field surrounding it, which can cause hum in an audio signal. If you must have AC and audio cables in close proximity, cross them at right angles rather than having them run along parallel paths. This minimizes the area of contact they'll have with each other.

❏ Dress your cable runs so that the area under your desk doesn't look like Medusa on a bad hair day. Group similar cables together, and separate cables that don't play nice (such as audio and power). You can use a loom, harness, special cable ties, or even low-tack masking tape (*low-tack* means it won't leave a residue, unlike duct tape) to bunch cables together. Stay away from bread and garbage-bag ties because the wires can break through the paper covering and cut into your cables' rubber insulation.

❏ Buy quality cables from music stores, not cheap ones from consumer electronics stores. Many large music stores have pro audio departments, and the sales personnel can advise you on the best cable for a particular function.

❏ Have tons of adapters around of all flavors (1/8" to 1/4", 1/4" to RCA, female-to-female extension cables, etc.) and keep them in an easily accessible place. They're cheap, simple, and they'll save your life (or at least your session).

Moving On

Now that your surroundings are warm and fuzzy and your audio is crystal clear, you should have no problems in producing great music in your studio. That is, unless something goes wrong. The true test of knowing your studio is how quickly you can diagnose and fix a problem when the equipment starts misbehaving. In Chapter 8 we'll look at squashing some common bugaboos that can creep into your studio and wreak havoc.

One Day at a Time

Start any construction project early in the morning so you can finish it in one day—or at least so you can control when you stop for the day.

At this point, you should have the following items completed:

- ❏ You made a detailed, written drawing of what the final arrangement of your studio will look like.

- ❏ You have all your raw materials for making baffles—lumber, hardware, and tools.

- ❏ You scoped out where and how the baffles will hang.

- ❏ You moved existing furniture around in a "dry run" before permanently setting up equipment.

- ❏ You have an assistant to help you with making and hanging the acoustic panels.

- ❏ You have an assistant to help you with turning off the electricity, if you're planning on replacing a light switch with a dimmer.

Chapter 8

Maintaining and Caring for Your Recording System

Protecting Your System and Your Data

Recording may be your life's passion, but to the computer, it's just another number-crunching task, like word processing, Web browsing, or gaming. So on one level, what's good for the computer in general is good for music and audio production. But audio recording and music production present the computer and its user with some special demands, so a specific approach is required toward three very important computing procedures: *maintenance, backup,* and *troubleshooting.* In this chapter, we'll tackle all three issues, offering tips for your computing routines and recommending specific tools to help make the job more seamless so that you can get back to the primary job of making music.

Maintenance

Although passing audio is not particularly stressful on keyboards, drum machines, and interfaces, it does work the internal components of a computer pretty hard. The hard drive is constantly active, writing files to disk and then reading them back into RAM. Additionally, audio applications create big files—bigger files than do word processors, games, image-editing programs, and many other programs. Bigger files mean more impact on your hard drive and more work for its mechanisms and other components. You can own an electronic keyboard and a microphone and never have to service them, but your computer requires constant maintenance.

Now before you get anxious about the word "maintenance," this is not like having to bring your computer into the shop every couple weeks for an oil change. All the maintenance you can perform yourself using software. The only hard part is remembering to do it. You'll have to bring your computer in *only* if you have a hardware problem (or a *really* vexing software problem masquerading as a hardware problem), which is rare. Most problems that seem like hardware are really software problems in disguise.

Creating Partitions

Setting up your computer so that it runs correctly in the first place is the best insurance against many of the problems that can occur later on. One of the first things you should do when preparing a computer for music production is to *partition your hard drive.* Though not a completely secure way to protect your files from component failure, it is a good-housekeeping habit for audio production.

Partitioning is where you use software to create "boundaries" on your physical hard drive, breaking it up into smaller "virtual" drives, which then appear as individual volumes (icons) on your desktop. This allows you to perform maintenance and backup operations on them, as if they were separate drives. It often helps to isolate files from a partition that may be having problems, creating a sort of "data quarantine."

When you buy an already-assembled, working computer (called a "system" by the technically inclined), you usually get a hard drive with no partitions (or one big one, depending on how you look at it). You then use software to create two or more smaller partitions. If you're setting up a new hard drive or are reformatting an existing one, you can choose to create partitions at the time you format, or *initialize,* the disk.

Figure 8-1 shows a setup screen from PowerQuest's PartitionMagic, a popular and easy-to-use program for partitioning your hard drive. Note that the partitions you create bear letters (E, F, G, etc.) just like the physical drives in your system.

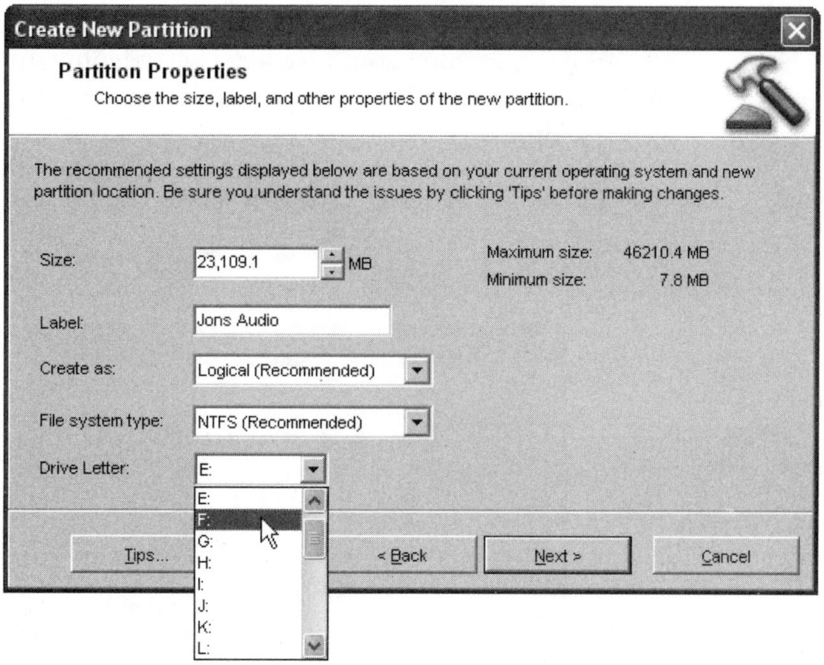

Figure 8-1
Partitioning your hard drive produces "virtual" drives, each of which appears as a separate icon on the desktop. This allows you to perform maintenance and backup routines on them individually.

The more capacious hard drives get, the more sense it makes to partition them. If you picture your hard drive as a big lake, and you're responsible for monitoring the lake's activities, your job will be a whole lot more manageable if you put swimmers in one area, ski boats in another, and non-motorized fishing boats in a third location. That way, you can keep similar activities together and not have swimmers getting bonked by skiers.

It works the same way with hard drive partitions. Good computing practice dictates that you partition your drive (or drives) when performing industrial-strength tasks such as marathon audio production, keeping the operating system and applications on one partition, and the files created by them on another.

Running Disk-Repair Utilities

The easiest type of maintenance to perform is to run a disk-utility program that will check the health of your drives and their files on several levels. Both Windows and Mac computers include disk utilities in their operating systems that will scan the disk and repair file- and disk-based errors (if they're fixable). Third-party utilities such as those made Norton offer even more features and flexibility. You should regularly run disk utilities, and it makes sense to schedule these tasks right before you do a complete backup and archive.

However, as the program will warn you, running any kind of disk utility is a risk to your data, so you should back up your documents (the files created by the applications) just before you run the disk-repair utility and then perform a complete backup.

Figure 8-2 shows the main window of Norton Disk Doctor, which checks files, directory structures, and the disk's media for errors and then fixes the problems for you. It also generates a report, if you like to keep track of such things.

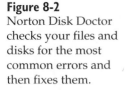

Figure 8-2
Norton Disk Doctor checks your files and disks for the most common errors and then fixes them.

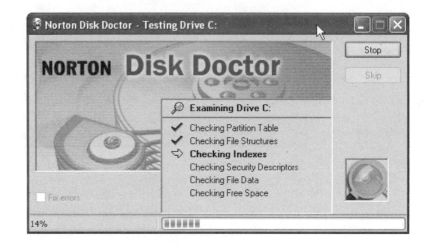

Virus Software

Not specific to music, but necessary for any computer that communicates with the outside world, is running virus-protection software. Most musicians regularly use the Internet for retrieving music files, sound effects, patches, shareware utilities, and e-mail and therefore are just as exposed to contracting a virus as other computer users. Macs aren't nearly as vulnerable to viruses as Windows machines are, simply because there are far fewer viruses written for the Mac OS (a virus written for Windows is harmless on a Mac, and vice versa), but all computer users, regardless of platform, should run virus-protection software. It's innocuous, runs in the background, and you have to shut it off only when installing some copy-protected software from the installation CD or when running a disk utility. Windows XP and Mac OS X, with their well-integrated Internet support for software updates, can alert you to new fixes. This is critical with virus-protection software because new viruses are, unfortunately, constantly being written and unleashed.

Defragmenting Your Disk

When you record music on your computer, data is written onto your hard disk. Normally the read/write apparatus places this data in connected, or *contiguous*, chunks. But as your drive fills up and old files get erased and new files get written, their data naturally gets separated, or *fragmented,* across the surface of the drive medium. This is usually okay, because when you go to read the file, the computer is fast enough to pick up the variously located bits and load them into RAM for a glitch-free playback. But if you have a seriously fragmented disk, your performance can be affected, and your hard drive works a lot harder than it has to, zipping around the disk to find all the fragments belonging to a particular file.

The periodic defragmenting of your hard disk reassembles all parts of a file next to each other for more efficient data reading, and it leaves larger sections of free space so that files saved after defragmenting aren't themselves fragmented.

Defragmenting is a fairly low-risk venture, as far disk routines go, but you should back up important files (if you haven't just done a complete disk backup) before engaging in any disk-based operation. To defragment in Windows, go to Programs | Accessories | System Tools | Disk Defragmenter and follow the prompts. (Mac users will have to use a third-party utility such as Norton Utilities because defragmenting is not included with the Mac OS.) It's a good idea to invoke the Analyze function first, just to see how fragmented your files are. Then just click Defragment and take a break because it's a time-consuming process.

Figure 8-3 shows the Defragmenting utility option from the Start menu in Windows XP. Always choose Analyze before performing the defragmenting process. This will help you monitor how fragmented your disk becomes during your recording practices.

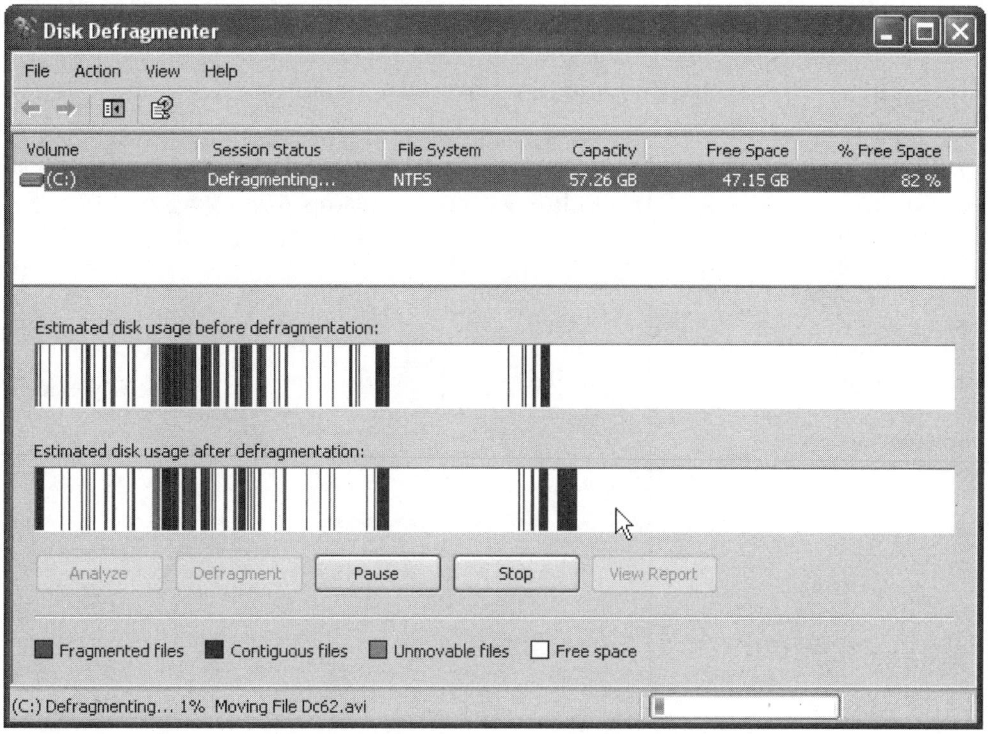

Figure 8-3
Defragmenting is one of the best things you can do to ensure smooth, glitch-free audio performance from your hard disk, and it's built right in to the operating systems of Windows.

Updating Software

As long as you have an Internet connection, updating software is fairly easy, especially with the newer operating systems of Mac OS X and Windows XP. There's the old adage that goes "If it ain't broke, don't fix it," but often upgraded software fixes something that you didn't even realize was broken when you bought it. It's just the nature of software to improve itself, and you should try to update whenever you can.

Mac OS X and Windows XP make it very easy to check the Internet for updated software (they can do it automatically, as long as you're online), but you have to examine carefully the "readme" file to see what the updates do; otherwise, you could conceivably introduce a problem that wasn't there before. Software manufacturers take great care to make sure updates are "backwardly compatible," but with everything being updated—including your operating system—you might run into the dreaded "compatibility" problem (see the sidebar titled "Compatibility Issues"). This is where any two items (software or hardware) work fine by themselves but run into irreconcilable differences when they have to share the same environment. To cover yourself, don't update during a deadline situation, but do so soon after you've submitted or completed your project.

Figure 8-4 shows the prompt in Windows XP that signals it has found a more recent version of resident software. You can elect to have your operating system (both Mac OS and Windows) continually scan the Internet for updates to your existing programs so that you'll never fall too far behind in updates (unless you choose to ignore the messages, of course).

Figure 8-4
A dialog box appears whenever Windows detects that a newer version of your software is available. Clicking in the affirmative will bring you to a Web page that allows you to execute the update process.

Compatibility Issues

Compatibility means that two or more components have to agree. When they don't, it's not necessarily the fault of one or the other but rather what happens when they get together. Compatibility can be tricky, because the blame doesn't squarely fall into one camp or the other—thus making it hard to know who should rewrite their code to make nice.

Compatibility for computer users typically strikes at the operating system level, and usually involves drivers. Making sure you keep a close watch on your operating system's developments and your audio manufacturers' efforts to keep up with the changing times is the best way to stay ahead of the compatibility race.

Whenever there's a major operating system upgrade, such as from Windows Me and Windows 2000 to Windows XP, or from Mac OS 9.x to OS X, software applications running on those platforms must undergo extensive rewriting. Efforts are made for backward compatibility, but sometimes a maker just has to cut its losses and start over (which is what happened in the Macintosh case, though Apple allows you to run 9.x under OS X, which it calls "Classic" mode). It is often a painful and expensive decision, but most people are aware that it is the price of progress and try to comply. And at least in the case of XP and OS X, the results are well worth it. Besides, it's a healthy thing to learn something new.

Lean, Mean Data Machines

Another good-housekeeping measure for hard disks is to regularly remove files you're not using anymore. Many sound and music vendors offer demo versions of their software, and it's a great thing to try them out for free. It encourages you to do a lot of downloading and installing. But once the demo expires or you decide not to use the program anymore, you should delete it and its attendant files. Though the application is usually the biggest space hog, it's a good idea to get rid of all the little files a program creates. Using the Remove Programs (which XP calls *Change or Remove Programs)* utility will get rid of the bulky program files and many of the attendant files, but it may not grab everything. Applying the Windows Disk Cleanup feature at regular intervals will help keep your hard drive clutter-free.

Figure 8-5 shows the screen for Windows Disk Cleanup. This utility shows you by category the files it deems safe to delete. Deleting Temporary Internet Files, Recycle Bin, and Temporary Files is a good place to start.

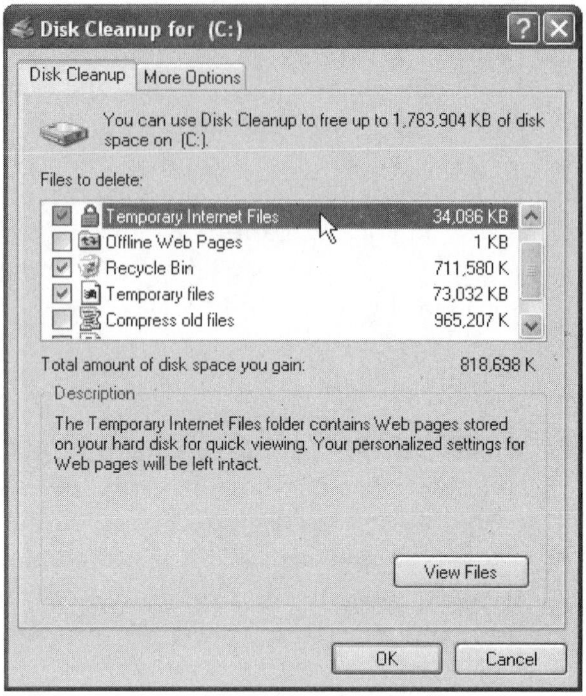

Figure 8-5
Windows Disk Cleanup lets you be selective in your file deletion, in case you're not sure you'll need certain files later on.

Keeping Components Clean and Happy

Music and audio production is a very clean endeavor, unlike working with automobile engines or in a restaurant kitchen. So it doesn't take much beyond placing your gear in the same environment that's safe and healthy for humans to keep your equipment happy.

Dust in the Wind

You should keep noncomputer musical gear such as keyboards and mixers covered with a dust cover. Dust can get inside the open cracks between keys and in the fader slots, which can cause corrosion on the contacts.

A layer of dust on the surface of your computer or monitor isn't bad for it *per se*, but that dust has a tendency to get into your lungs easier, and that *is* bad. Plus, it looks terrible to clients and collaborators. So keep the dust off of the surfaces of your components (especially the screen) by dusting them lightly occasionally and wiping with a damp cloth. Special antistatic wipes exist for glass monitors, and though they're not necessary for keeping a monitor clean, they're nice to have if you have regular visitors, or if you yourself are persnickety about having components that are all clean all the time.

Dust *inside* of your system can cause problems, though. When dust accumulates on the case's vents, blocked airflow can result, making your computer's interior heat up. Processors have been known to fail in high heat, so it's important to keep the vents dust-free so that air can flow freely and the fans can draw heat out of the computer's interior.

Use a can of compressed air on the exterior and interior of the vents to blow away all the dust. If you're careful, you can open the case and blow away even more dust from the motherboard's nook and crannies, but be careful not to touch or dislodge any components. Many computer technicians have adjustable-speed vacuums for gently drawing away the dust balls and tumbleweeds from the case's interior that collect from the effects of static electricity.

It's the Heat *and* the Humidity

Extreme heat is not good for computers for the same reasons it isn't good for humans: It causes overheating and meltdown (though with computers this has a more literal meaning). Although computers have internal fans to keep the air flowing and the exchange of heat going from hot interior to cooler room, that process becomes less effective as the room heats up along with the computer's insides. So keep your computer in a climate-controlled environment, especially if you keep it on for long periods of time.

Excess humidity isn't good for any electronic components either, including computers. If your climate-control system doesn't keep the humidity level between 45 and 55 percent, consider getting a dehumidifier if the humidity level rises above 55 percent. Dry environments won't hurt a computer, but they're not that healthy for their operators (that would be you), so if you use a humidifier to bring the level up to about 50 percent, the computer won't complain.

Once you've got the climate and the pollutants under control, you just need to protect your computer from injury. Because computing is a not a contact sport (unless you're *really* angry at your PC), the only physical damage it's in danger of suffering comes from the AC power. Audio and MIDI signals, which operate on the milliamp level, can't damage your components. The following section deals with taming potentially damaging AC power.

The Urge to Surge

A *surge protector* can be found inside many power strips, or you can buy a higher-quality one in the form of a *line conditioner*, a 1RU box that offers other functions, including power conditioning and filtering. A surge protector prevents unpredictable voltage spikes from damaging the sensitive components of your gear or wiping out your computer's memory. The computer's power supply is capable of handling moderate power fluctuations, but a surge protector is extra insurance against drastic voltage spikes.

Don't Interrupt when I'm Powering

A UPS (*you-pea-ess*), in computer terms, does not denote the reliable brown-uniformed delivery service but rather an *uninterruptible power supply*. It comes in the form of a box, a little smaller than a computer tower, and sits between the wall outlet and your computer. A UPS also includes a surge protector, but its chief feature is not fending off too much voltage, but what it does when faced with the opposite situation.

When the power to your computer dips below a certain level—or fails completely in a total blackout—your UPS steps up to the plate with battery power and allows you enough time to save your work safely to disk and shut down all your gear. If you live in an area where power is unreliable or storms regularly knock out the power, you should get a UPS. Its chief features are as follows:

❑ Provides power during a blackout

❑ Boosts power to the proper level during a sag

❑ Absorbs power surges

❑ Filters noisy power sources

You can hook up a lot of gear to your UPS, because it features many outlets. It's also a good idea to attach any microprocessor-controlled device, such as your keyboard workstation, so that your internal memory doesn't get zapped or corrupted during a power sag or surge.

Figure 8-6 shows a typical UPS with lots of stuff plugged in. You don't have to have easy access to it, because once you plug into it, you're pretty much done. So you can stash it in an out-of-the-way location, such as under a desk.

Figure 8-6
An uninterruptible power supply (UPS) is about the size of a fishing-tackle box and is the best insurance against an unpredictable power source.

Backing Up

Everyone these days understands the importance of backing up files, even if we don't do it as much as we should. Data living on a hard disk is a fairly stable situation, but it is possible to upset that stability. Your computer doesn't have to blow up in a puff of blue smoke to signal a catastrophic event, and a hard drive doesn't have to "break down" to wreak havoc on your creations. It has to fail only just enough to corrupt a tiny string of ones and zeros to turn a file into gibberish.

As storage media get cheaper and cheaper, and as software increasingly makes the process less painful, there's more incentive than ever to do what's actually good for us. In this section, we'll look at the different backup solutions available and explore a couple strategies for preserving the single most valuable asset in your studio: the files you create.

Backup Basics: Diversifying Disks

The first step to backing up is having more than one place to put your data. Using two or more hard disks is better than partitioning a single disk (described earlier in the chapter) because it allows you to put your data on separate *devices*. Although there are advantages to having partitions on a drive versus not having partitions (you can format, defrag, and perform other routines on just a partition rather than the whole drive), nothing beats having two separate physical drives for data redundancy (which is a good thing).

The advantages of having two drives are as follows:

- ❑ Data is kept on two physical devices, so if one fails, the other will still work.

- ❑ The second drive can be physically moved, hooked up to another machine, or replaced.

- ❑ Data integrity is better preserved on a second, "document-only" drive, because numerous and miscellaneous files are not written to it as often as the startup drive, which contains the operating system and applications.

It used to be that the benefit of having a second drive included having more storage space than your primary drive could supply. But now, with such large and affordable hard drives available (and the price of removable-media drives coming down), that's not as an important a factor (though it's still certainly true) as the other data-redundancy advantages of having two separate drives.

In fact, just because you have a large drive doesn't mean you should fill it. It's healthy for a drive to have plenty of open space, or working room. The motivation for a second drive should come long before you run out of room on the first. When people ask me about acquiring large hard drives, I try to make sure they're doing it for the right reasons, and not just for the capacity. I try to instill the notion that it's not good to put all your eggs in one basket.

After a point, it doesn't make sense to buy larger and larger hard drives, just so you can keep all your data in one place. At least from a data-security perspective, two 80GB drives are better than one 160GB drive. Because, after all, how much data are you willing to lose in one shot?

Moving Forward with Backing Up

Simply making two copies of your data isn't the most rigorous approach to backing up your data safely. Many data preservationists feel that data isn't really backed up unless it's saved onto two *different* types of media, because problems that occur on one device can often spread to other devices of the same type. So other than having a hard drive or two, invest in plenty of blank CD-R or CD-RW discs, because burning data (not audio) to these inexpensive media is a good way to get in the habit of creating backups. If you simply burn your files to a CD-R after every session, you're performing a reasonably safe backup routine.

Also, don't confuse backing up with archiving. *Archiving* is storing data after you're finished with it. Backing up is for active work that you need to access quickly. Archives are often compressed and may exist as the only copy, but it's a good idea to back up an archive copy, too. A true backup file, however, shouldn't be compressed at all; it should be an exact copy of the working file.

Making a copy of your data in two locations just makes good sense. But there are certain advantages in each type of media. Let's take a look at the available options.

Media Types

These days, you can back up to anything from a floppy disk, to a high-end tape drive, to a number of choices in between. Each type of media has inherent strengths and limitations with regard to backup routines, so let's see what's available and examine their attributes.

Floppy Disk

Not usable for audio, but at 1.4MB capacity, a floppy disk is enough to hold a project file from an audio sequencer or to accommodate MIDI files (which require much less storage space than audio). The advantage is that all PC computers have a floppy drive, but floppy disks are not considered a real backup medium for audio work. Use them for small files and only when no other option is available (such as when you're on the road with a laptop).

CD-R/CD-RW

These writeable discs hold up to 700MB of data, which is enough for about 140 track minutes (mono) of CD-quality, 16-bit/44.1 kHz audio, or 70 minutes for two channels of stereo (actually you can squeeze a bit more onto CDs, and commercial manufacturers can get up to 80 minutes). Put another way, you can get about 20 three-and-a-half-minute songs (in stereo) on a single CD-R.

CD-Rs are cheap, less than a dollar apiece, and they write faster than CD-RWs, so they're handy when you need to back up in a hurry. CD-RWs are rewriteable and therefore make a better choice for backup than CD-Rs in general. If you work on the song level, where each project contains files associated with songs that are about 3.5 minutes in length and don't contain more than eight full tracks of audio, you can use a CD-R to back up your data.

If you need more storage space than that, you'll have to divide your audio files across several discs, so choose an organization scheme that makes sense to you, such as storing each individual audio and MIDI track, instrument, or group of instruments on its own CD. Determining storage space is a simple matter of converting megabytes to minutes. At the CD standard (16-bit/44.1 kHz), each minute of audio requires about 5MB of disk space. One minute of stereo audio requires 10MB, and a stereo (two-track) mixdown of a three-and-a-half-minute pop song requires about 35MB.

Table 8-1 shows a chart with the most common audio resolution formats and the amount of storage space required per track minute at that resolution. Additional columns provide typical times and track groupings for the most common types of projects.

Equating Resolution and Megabytes per Minute

Bit Depth	Sample Rate	MB per Minute	Stereo/ 5 Minutes	8 Tracks/ 10 Minutes	16 Tracks/ 20 Minutes
16	44.1 kHz	5.0MB	50MB	400MB	1.6GB
16	48 kHz	5.5MB	55MB	440MB	1.76GB
24	44.1 kHz	7.6MB	76MB	608MB	2.43GB
24	48 kHz	8.25MB	82.5MB	660MB	2.64GB
24	96 kHz	16.5MB	165MB	1.32GB	5.28GB

Table 8-1
At 16-bit/44.1 kHz, the CD audio standard, 5MB per track minute is required for storage space. A stereo mixdown requires 10MB per minute, so a five-minute song requires about 50MB of disk space.

DVD

Though more expensive than CD-RWs, a DVD holds more than six times the amount of data (4.7GB) and is therefore very appealing to musicians, even beyond their capacity to accommodate video. The capacity of a DVD is 4.7GB, or 9GB for a two-sided DVD. DVD burners come in two formats: DVD+RW and DVD-RW, so be careful which one you choose if you need to interact with other DVD users. If you're using the drive only for yourself, then it doesn't matter because you'll be reading and writing from the same drive. Apple uses the DVD-RW format on the computers it produces with built-in DVD burners.

External DVD burners now cost about $250 and can be connected to your existing computer through FireWire or SCSI. This is a good alternative to the true "removable media" solution (see the section entitled "Removable Disks") because you can move the DVD burner around to various computers, assuming you have a SCSI or FireWire card on them.

Magneto-Optical

Magneto-Optical (M-O) is a very stable and robust format because it writes using optical technology, which is immune to magnetic corruption, and reads using magnetic technology, which is fast and inexpensive. M-O isn't as popular as it once was, and it's being eclipsed by other formats. However, it's still a completely viable backup solution, assuming you have access to the media and a good, working M-O drive.

Tape Drives

Tape is very economical because DAT/DDS cassettes can hold up to 50MB of uncompressed data and 100MB of compressed data. However, tape drives record and play back linearly, which is a time-consuming process. Tape drives are used extensively in business environments, and the blank media are readily available, but they tend not to be popular with musicians or owner-operated studios. The newest technology in tape backup, Advanced Intelligence Tape (AIT), gets around the linear limitation somewhat by creating a file directory that it keeps in memory, allowing faster access.

Removable Disks

The ubiquitous 100MB Zip drive, by Iomega, belongs to the category known as *removable storage media*. Although a Zip disk holds only about 100MB of data (it's actually more like 96MB), that can be enough for a couple of songs or several tracks of a project in progress. The 250MB Zip drive will read and write disks two-and-half times larger than the 100MB model, plus it reads and writes the standard 100MB disks as well. For smaller projects, and for interacting with people who have other Zip drives, this is a viable solution.

The Peerless, also by Iomega, is a removable hard disk and mechanism available in several configurations, such as the 20GB model. Because it's removable, the media is separate from the mechanism itself and is more versatile than, say, an external hard drive. The mechanism is designed so that the hard disk caddies slip in and out of the drive mechanism easily. Hard disk technology has the advantage over cartridges in that they're much faster in matters of random access and can hold much more data.

Straddling the line between removable media and external hard drives are USB- and FireWire-based enclosures, which allow you to freely swap out standard IDE (or ATA/ATAPI) hard drives. Because these drives are inexpensive and plentiful, an enclosure approach is very appealing from an economic perspective. Figure 8-7 shows a ClearLight enclosure drive, which offers a choice of USB or FireWire ports for connecting to the computer. The IDE drive is visible through the translucent case.

Figure 8-7
The enclosure system features a housing that connects to the computer via USB or FireWire and allows you to easily add and remove standard IDE (ATA/ATAPI) drives.

Internal and External Hard Drives

The cost of hard drive technology keeps going down as its speed and capacity rise, so whether you opt for an internal or external version, it's hard to beat a standard hard drive for reliability, convenience, and value. If you don't have a second drive inside your computer, you should add one; they're cheaper than their external counterparts because you don't have to pay for the housing and power-supply circuitry (they run off the existing components already inside your computer).

Your second internal drive can be used in one of two ways: to store project files only (while the operating system and applications reside on the primary drive) or as a *mirror* (exact copy) of your startup drive. If you decide to use your second drive as a mirror, make sure it's configured to be bootable so that if your primary startup drive fails, you not only have your all your data intact, but you can boot up from the second drive as well. Internal drives can be difficult to access physically once they become full or you want to use them with a different computer, so it's not quite as versatile as an external hard drive, but it's recommended that all audio users have at least two internal hard drives.

External hard drives can connect to the computer via USB, SCSI, and FireWire and are more easily interchangeable between computers than internal drives. All computers these days come with built-in USB, so for strictly backup purposes (where data-transfer speed is not an issue), an external USB hard drive is a very attractive solution. FireWire comes built in to Macs and is available on a PCI card option for about $60 for PCs that don't have them. A SCSI drive requires that you have a PCI-based SCSI card, but the advantage here is that modern SCSI formats are faster than USB and FireWire. An external SCSI drive can be used like an internal drive in that it's fast enough for capturing audio on the fly. As of this writing, an external 80GB drive is about $200.

Backup Software

Backing up is such an integral part of computing that specially designed software exists to help you manage your backup routines. Programs such as Dantz's Retrospect and NewTech Infosystems' Backup Now! are excellent backup utilities that will back up your hard drive onto several types of media. They can automate the process, starting the backup routine (and the restore routine, if necessary) at scheduled intervals. This allows you to set the time for, say, 4:00 in the morning, when you're asleep. Of course, this means you have to have your computer on at that time, and most home users still prefer to shut their computers off for the night.

Figure 8-8 shows a screen from Dantz's Retrospect Express Scheduling wizard, which allows you to establish what kind of media you'll use, how often you want to back up, how many copies you'd like, and the time of day you'd like the backup process to begin.

But scheduling regular backup routines is a way to ensure that it actually gets

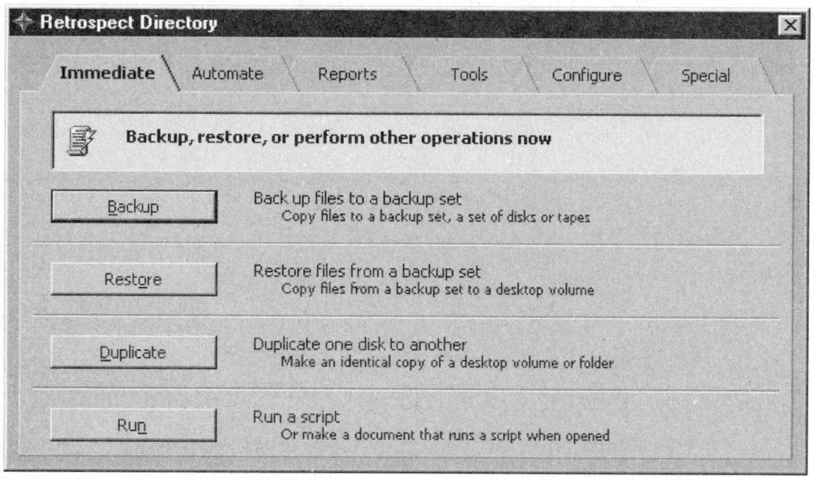

Figure 8-8
Dantz's Retrospect Express is a popular backup program that allows you to automate your backup routine with a great degree of control and versatility.

done, because if left to our own devices, most of us wouldn't get into the habit of backing up as assiduously as we should. I usually do a full backup to DVD once a week, but during the week I copy any working files to my external hard drive at the end of the day, using a "smart merge" approach. *Smart merge* means the copy utility looks at the "source" folder containing all my documents and compares it to the "destination" folder containing the backup. It then copies *only* new files and files changed since the last smart merge (one day, if I've kept on schedule).

Synchronizing data means the computer will compare two versions of a document or folder and keep only the one with the newer date, overwriting the older one to match the newer one. This allows you to work with two machines, such as a laptop and desktop, where you'll be making changes from both machines. Smart merge is best used for one-way backing up (such as from your computer to a removable media device), whereas synchronizing allows for bidirectional work, such as when you're working on the road as well as at home.

Troubleshooting

Because you have many processes going on inside your computer, and at least a couple devices hanging off of it, it's sometimes confusing to know exactly where a problem is occurring. For the most basic problem—no sound—it could be anything from not having your mic or guitar plugged in all the way (or at all—we've all been there!) to having the volume on your speakers turned down. Or anything in between.

The trick is not only to diagnose a problem but to do it quickly and systematically. Following is a handy checklist you can use to quickly determine exactly where a problem lies, plus the suggestions that may fix the most likely cause. For a more detailed description on troubleshooting device-driver conflicts and other audio issues, see the descriptions following the checklist.

Troubleshooting Checklist

Is there sound through the speakers?

If not, check the volume level, AC power, and audio connections. If the speakers are working, you should hear a slight hum when you turn the volume all the way up.

Can the computer play system sounds?

If not, it means sound isn't getting out of the computer at all, and it's probably not the application. Check the application's I/O configuration, the devices, and the drivers.

Can the CD drive play audio?

If not, and you're not receiving error messages, try reinstalling the device driver or checking for an updated driver online.

Does your MP3 player produce audio?

Because your MP3 player is closely tied to your operating system, using it to check audio helps to delineate problems between software and devices. If your MP3 player appears to play but can't produce audio, you probably have a problem on the device level.

Do other applications play sound?

If so, it means your devices are passing audio, and it's a configuration error within the problem application, or it's a driver issue between the application and the device. If not, the problem may lie with the device. If you're using an audio program to test internal sounds, make sure you reset the audio engine to access the system sounds.

Does switching devices solve the problem?

If you can produce audio from, say, your computer's integrated audio system but not the soundcard, the problem lies within the application and its communication with the device. If switching devices doesn't produce audio, the problem might be a driver configuration issue, so try switching driver types (e.g., from ASIO to Audio Units or WDM).

Do both audio and MIDI files play?

If not, check the routing of the problem file type and try changing it to a different device to better determine the source of the problem.

Are there driver duplicates or conflicts?

If so, try removing and reinstalling all the drivers. Before doing this, make sure you have the installation CD handy or have copied the drivers from the manufacturer's Web site to a directory on your hard drive.

Does the application crash on startup, when opening a file, or during any task?

If so, try reinstalling the application from the installation CD.

Delving Deeper into the Root of Audio Problems

One of the most common problems for audio is the communication of the software to the hardware. When the software is functioning properly and the devices are in working order, yet there's still no sound, the problem can usually be traced to a configuration error. This could be anything from settings in the software to a driver conflict.

Fortunately, Windows XP's excellent help and troubleshooting guides make it a snap to resolve conflicts on the system level (drivers, devices, IRQ conflicts, etc.). For general audio, entertainment, and device questions, check out the "troubleshooter" tool at Start | Help and Support Center | Fixing a Problem | Troubleshooting Problems | List of Troubleshooters. Here you'll see a list of topics that pertain to whatever device you suspect might be giving you trouble.

Figure 8-9 shows some of the typical situations, presented in the form of first-person statements by you, the user, from the Windows troubleshooter tool. When you're having a problem, look for the statement that most closely resembles your problem (e.g., "A sound appears to play, but I do not hear anything."). You'll then be directed to suggested steps, including the opening of certain windows, which you can do right from the tool via links. You're then asked whether this solved the problem. If you answer no, you're given an alternate course.

Figure 8-9
Windows XP's troubleshooter tool asks a series of questions or presents a series of statements that helps you determine and then troubleshoot your particular problem.

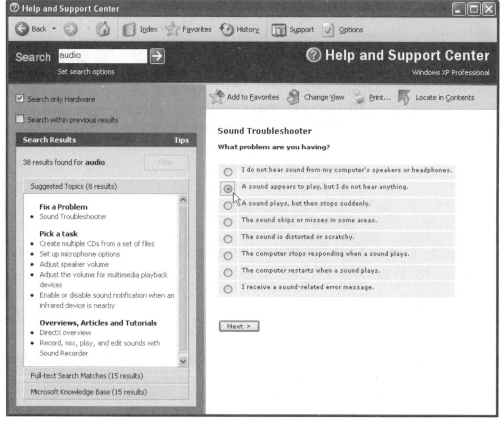

Use the troubleshooter tool before resorting to calling the tech support departments of the software or hardware manufacturers. I've found that its thorough and systematic checks solve almost all configuration problems that occur between the Windows operating system and the software and devices.

Windows XP's troubleshooter is an excellent way to hierarchically step through a question-and-answer format to drill down to the specifics of an audio problem, but here are the steps to take for the most common scenarios musicians working with soundcards, audio peripherals, and higher-end audio programs will encounter.

What to do when there's no sound

Check whether all components that should be on are on and that power cables are secure (most pro gear uses a detachable power cord, which is a good thing, but it can jiggle loose over time). Check to see that all audio, MIDI, and other data connections are in place.

Do you hear *any* audio? For example, if you hear low-level white noise out of the speakers when you (carefully) turn up the volume (which indicates the speakers are on), you know that the problem lies further back in the chain.

Can you hear a system beep sound? To determine if your computer is capable of producing sound, try playing a system sound through the speakers or headphones. Open Start | Control Panel | Sounds and Audio Devices Properties | Volume and then drag the Device volume slider to the right or left (with Mute unchecked). When you release the mouse button, you should hear a beep. If you don't, check your speaker, headphone, or external audio connections.

If you can hear a beep, the next step is to make sure all your volume settings are turned up for the different types of sounds. Open Start | All Programs | Accessories | Entertainment | Volume and then move all the sliders about three-quarters of the way up and make sure all the Mute switches are unchecked and the Balance sliders are centered.

What to do when the sound is noisy

First, determine the quality of the sound. Is it a low, steady hum (which would indicate a ground loop), or is it crackly and sporadic (indicating shorting)?

If it's a hum, check all audio cable connections to make sure they're inserted all the way in. Try changing the location of your AC plugs. Place all of them into one power strip rather than having them feed into different power strips that go into different wall sockets. If the sound is crackling and sporadic, indicating momentary shorting to ground, try twisting or jiggling the plugs to get rid of the crackling sound, if only momentarily, to determine if the problem is in the audio connections. If you have a persistent ground problem, you may have to call in a licensed electrician. He or she can check out your equipment, trace the wiring in the household, and rewire your outlets, if necessary.

What to do when the sound is distorted or overdriven

Check to see that your volume levels are not too high throughout the signal chain. Distortion can result if your multimedia speakers are turned way down and you turn your up system volume to compensate. The opposite situation, where your speakers are too high and you've turned down your system volume, will also produce noisy sound. Do a systematic check of all levels before making any adjustments. If you must adjust something, make sure you're turning it down, to protect your ears and speakers from levels that are too high.

What to do when playback starts but then stops

If you're having this problem with a CD drive, check to see that you have the latest driver for your operating system.

If you're having this problem with a file on your hard disk, check to see that your buffer settings match the software's recommended settings. Make a note of your current settings and try increasing the size of the buffer. This will improve latency but may reduce overall system performance. For now, though, you just want to see if you can play uninterrupted audio.

If the buffer settings are okay, check the troubleshooters (in Windows) to see if there are any driver problems or hardware conflicts. Often a correction in these areas requires a restart.

What to do when the sound plays but there are skips and dropouts

In Windows XP, open Start | Control Panel | Sounds and Audio Devices Properties | Hardware and then select the current device. Next, select Properties | Driver | Driver Details and select the associated driver from that list. Check that the "Digital Signer" includes an entry and not "Not digitally signed." If your device is not digitally signed, try to get an updated driver from the manufacturer.

What to do when the computer stops responding when a sound plays

Try playing a different type of file. For example, if the computer halts when playing an audio file, try playing just a MIDI file, and vice versa. If the problem persists with both types of files, you may have a device (or hardware) conflict, where two devices are trying to use the same resource or IRQ (*interrupt request line*, a hardware line over which devices send messages to the processor).

In Windows XP, open Control Panel | System | Hardware | Device Manager | Sound, Video and Game Controllers. If you see a red X, that means the device is off. To turn it on, under Device Manager, right-click the device marked with the X and select Properties. Select Device Usage and then select Use This Device (Enable) and click OK. Restart your computer.

If you see an exclamation point in a yellow circle, this indicates a conflict. To resolve a conflict, check the Device Manager to see if your device is listed twice. If so, delete (by right-clicking and selecting Uninstall) *all* occurrences of that device. Then restart your computer, which will cause Windows to detect a new device. Follow the prompts for reinstalling the device, including loading the drivers anew from the installation CD that came with the device. If you're installing an updated driver from the Internet, make sure it's already downloaded and stored in a directory on your hard drive. Alternatively, you can install the device manually by using the Add Hardware wizard in the Control Panel.

Moving On

By completing the three parts of *Build Your Own PC Recording Studio*, you have successfully negotiated the basic steps in the world of professional recording—all through your home computer. Armed with the principles laid out in this book, you're now free to venture further down any path you encountered on this journey.

Your audio and MIDI software has countless features that help in music making, but the best way to become more expert in the recording process has little to do with technology and everything to do with experience; you simply have to record over and over to become better at it. Your ability to work the software, along with the other tools in your studio, will naturally improve—just as practicing an instrument improves your musicianship.

Consider that the Beatles recorded their landmark album, *Sgt. Pepper's Lonely Hearts Club Band*, on a crude (by today's standards) four-track, reel-to-reel machine. What made those songs great and that album such a fabulous listening experience was not the technology, but the musicianship in the songs and the incentiveness that the artists showed using the tools at hand. You may feel you're struggling to learn your system now, but keep recording and your equipment will be scrambling to keep up with you. Just be sure to keep your gear busy capturing, editing, and burning all your creative impulses.

Index

INTERNATIONAL CONTACT INFORMATION

AUSTRALIA
McGraw-Hill Book Company Australia Pty. Ltd.
TEL +61-2-9900-1800
FAX +61-2-9878-8881
http://www.mcgraw-hill.com.au
books-it_sydney@mcgraw-hill.com

CANADA
McGraw-Hill Ryerson Ltd.
TEL +905-430-5000
FAX +905-430-5020
http://www.mcgraw-hill.ca

GREECE, MIDDLE EAST, & AFRICA
(Excluding South Africa)
McGraw-Hill Hellas
TEL +30-210-6560-990
TEL +30-210-6560-993
TEL +30-210-6560-994
FAX +30-210-6545-525

MEXICO (Also serving Latin America)
McGraw-Hill Interamericana Editores S.A. de C.V.
TEL +525-117-1583
FAX +525-117-1589
http://www.mcgraw-hill.com.mx
fernando_castellanos@mcgraw-hill.com

SINGAPORE (Serving Asia)
McGraw-Hill Book Company
TEL +65-6863-1580
FAX +65-6862-3354
http://www.mcgraw-hill.com.sg
mghasia@mcgraw-hill.com

SOUTH AFRICA
McGraw-Hill South Africa
TEL +27-11-622-7512
FAX +27-11-622-9045
robyn_swanepoel@mcgraw-hill.com

SPAIN
McGraw-Hill/Interamericana de España, S.A.U.
TEL +34-91-180-3000
FAX +34-91-372-8513
http://www.mcgraw-hill.es
professional@mcgraw-hill.es

UNITED KINGDOM, NORTHERN,
EASTERN, & CENTRAL EUROPE
McGraw-Hill Education Europe
TEL +44-1-628-502500
FAX +44-1-628-770224
http://www.mcgraw-hill.co.uk
computing_europe@mcgraw-hill.com

ALL OTHER INQUIRIES Contact:
McGraw-Hill/Osborne
TEL +1-510-596-6600
FAX +1-510-596-7600
http://www.osborne.com
omg_international@mcgraw-hill.com